S0-AAD-218

the
day
that
changed
the
world
Jon Paulien

Seeking God After September 11

REVIEW AND HERALD® PUBLISHING ASSOCIATION
HAGERSTOWN, MD 21740

Other books by Jon Paulien:

Knowing God in the Real World
The Millennium Bug
Present Truth in the Real World
What the Bible Says About the End-time

To order, call 1-800-765-6955.
Visit us at www.reviewandherald.com for
information on other Review and Herald® products.

Copyright © 2002 by
Review and Herald® Publishing Association
All rights reserved

The author assumes full responsibility for the accuracy of all facts
and quotations as cited in this book.

Unless otherwise noted, all Bible texts are from the *Holy Bible,
New International Version.* Copyright © 1973, 1978, 1984,
International Bible Society. Used by permission of Zondervan Bible
Publishers.

Bible texts credited to RSV are from the Revised Standard
Version of the Bible, copyright © 1946, 1952, 1971, by the Division
of Christian Education of the National Council of the Churches of
Christ in the U.S.A. Used by permission.

This book was
Edited by Gerald Wheeler
Copyedited by Jocelyn Fay and James Cavil
Designed by Genesis Design
Cover art by Aris Economopolis/Star-Ledger
Typeset: Times New Roman 10.5/12.5

PRINTED IN U.S.A.

06 05 04 03 02   5 4 3 2 1

R&H Cataloging Service
Paulien, Jonathan Karl, 1949-
    The day that changed the world.

    1. September Terror Attack, 2001. 2. Terrorism—Religious
aspects. 3. God. 4. Islam—Relations—Christianity. 5. Islamic fundamentalism. I. Title.

                    231.8

ISBN 0-8280-1754-9

I dedicate this book
to a dear friend and trusted adviser,
Samir Selmanovic.

His unique insights into Islam, the
contemporary secular scene in Manhattan,
and postmodern attitudes toward religion have
immeasurably enriched this book. I look forward
to the day when he will write a better one.

PREFACE

September 11, 2001, was more than just attacks on the World Trade Center in New York City. It also involved a strike on the Pentagon and an unknown target, probably either the White House or Congress. The latter two aspects of September 11 receive no attention in this book. But I do not in any way wish to minimize the suffering of victims and their families at the Pentagon or in the crash of Flight 93 in Shanksville, Pennsylvania. These events deserve books of their own. I simply decided to write a book that would focus exclusively on the World Trade Center attacks.

I have at least two reasons for this.

1. To a degree, the planes that crashed into the Pentagon and a field in Pennsylvania represent failures on the part of those who plotted the attacks. It seems likely that neither airplane struck its intended target (the pilot of the plane that crashed into the Pentagon seemed to have been searching for something else first), and the plane that hit the Pentagon did not do so in a way to cause maximum damage. Things could have been much worse. We will probably never know the degree to which heroic passengers or crew prevented both planes from causing a level of destruction comparable to that of the World Trade Center.

2. I know relatively little about the Washington, D.C., area or the workings of the Pentagon. Born and raised in New York City, though, I am thoroughly familiar with the towers and know many people affected by the attacks on New York. Thus the New York side of the tragedy particularly affected me. So it made sense for me to write about things that I knew something about. I hope that people touched by the other events of that day will find the bigger picture I present here helpful as well. Others will be able to fill in the gaps this book leaves behind.

CONTENTS

Preface

1

THE DAY THAT CHANGED THE WORLD

A little after 9:00 a.m. David glanced at his watch. An airplane had just struck the north tower of the World Trade Center. From his viewpoint on the upper floors of the south tower he could see black smoke pouring out of the impact area and drifting toward the east. People in the south tower immediately began to evacuate the skyscraper as a precaution. But David calculated that it would take at least an hour to inch down to the ground in the already-crowded stairwells of the south tower. Instead, he hit the elevator button. The doors opened. People in the lobby behind him shook their heads.

David didn't have time to explain. *If the accident is really limited to the north tower,* he thought, *the elevators in the south tower should be fully functional.* He got into the elevator with several others, but it remained half empty. As the elevator paused for a moment at the seventy-eighth floor, the second jetliner was about 60 seconds from impact. Spotting a woman friend, he asked her to join him.

"No," she said, "I want to stay here and watch over the other people."

"Well, good luck to you."

"Good luck to you, too," she responded.

It was the last time he would ever see her. As the half-empty elevator's doors closed, David would never forget the image of all those faces staring at him. Back at his apartment, 11 blocks north of the World Trade Center, he watched the two smoldering towers. He didn't realize that the wingtip of the second airplane had already ripped through the seventy-eighth floor elevator lobby, wreaking havoc among his former officemates. Although he had just come from the towers, it was hard to believe what he was seeing. Even as the south tower came down, he turned his head to the left and watched the scene unfold simultaneously on the television, as if to verify that what he saw outside his window was really happening. Reality and fantasy seemed to have become one.

A short time later and dazed with shock, Paul watched the screen of his television from the safety of Europe. Time and again CNN showed video of the second airliner approaching from the south and embedding itself completely into the south tower of the World Trade Center, the tower David had just evacuated. Again and again, from a different angle, he saw the massive fireball that exploded out of the other side of the tower, producing a shower of debris that floated downward like particles of dust. In the background of the video clips you could hear cries of horror as the scenes flashed before the eyes of people whose necks ached with the pain of looking constantly upward. As television played and replayed the scenes, news commentators rehashed what little information they knew in the hours immediately after the attack.

Paul thought of the tens of thousands of people who entered the towers on any given day. Soon it became evident that many on the top floors would not escape. While escape routes to the roof were clearly marked on the upper floors of the two towers, the smoke was so thick that rescue helicopters could not approach. As the fires spread, the heat became too painful to endure. Many chose the only alternative open to them, jumping through broken windows or off the roofs of the towers.

Much too soon the south tower gave way in a huge cloud of dust that obscured the fact that the whole structure had collapsed onto itself and essentially disappeared. Paul kept staring at the giant cloud, expecting the south tower to emerge into view again when the dust dissipated. Any hope he had left was dashed as the north tower, peeking out from the top of the dust cloud, crumpled 30 minutes later.

Then the television began presenting more personal images: men in white shirts and ties, carrying bags; girls in jeans; police in uniform. Suddenly all began racing away from the cyclone cloud of death, running for their lives, gasping for breath, terror in their eyes. Soon after came other images from hell. A man in a business suit using his tie as a filter in order to breathe. A woman with earrings and pearls around her neck, boots covered with dust, her mouth open— a dark gaping hole in her ashen face—hands spread apart, eyes terror-stricken. Dirty, bleeding survivors trudging toward where? Home? The company's other office? A friend's place?

What television could not share effectively were the sounds, the feel, the taste, and the smell of September 11. The video clips offered some sense of the screams and the cries of panic and terror that accompanied the collapse of the towers, but they could not capture the deafening roar, the trembling of the ground, and above all the taste of death. Those who were there say that you could taste the air more easily than you could breathe it. Even weeks later the acrid smell emanating from ground zero was nauseating. And in the middle of it all came the realization that burning human flesh was a part of the mix.

After the collapse of the two towers things quieted down. CNN kept repeating the same video clips. As reality began to sink in, Paul found himself particularly riveted by the image of the second plane approaching from the south, dipping its wings to the left at the last second, and disappearing into the south tower. As he viewed it again and again he felt an urge to reach out into the screen, grab hold of the plane, and save the towers and their occupants. *Is that what God must be feeling?* he suddenly thought to himself. *Did God want to prevent this as much as I do? Was He* unable *to stop it? Did He* decide *not to intervene? Was He there at all?* Paul found his thoughts getting more and more confused.

While the events of September 11 threw Paul's thoughts into confusion, others found themselves seeking God for the first time. As Paul watched the events unfold on his television set and David was looking out of his apartment window, others turned to Internet chat rooms, trying to make sense of the unfolding events. *Yahoo! Internet Life* magazine reported the following exchange of comments. The first plane crashed into the north tower about 8:45 a.m. and the second about 17 minutes later.

8:58 a.m.: "Plane crashes into the World Trade Center. Apologies for not linking to anything besides the main CNN page, but there are no full stories on this yet. The plane crashed into the building about six minutes ago, from what the TV is saying. We are about 60 blocks north and we can see the smoke over the skyline."—karen.

9:06 a.m.: "I'm looking at it right now (we can see the WTC from our office), and it looks like a second plane just hit the second tower (we just saw it happen). I can't confirm it, but it's absolutely crazy."—TNLNYC.

9:14 a.m.: "CNN is now reporting a second plane crash—one is a disaster, but two seems like it must be an attack to me."—mike.

9:15 a.m.: "This was no accident. No way."—ColdChef.

9:17 a.m.: "There's speculation that one of the planes was hijacked. . . . It gets worse every second."—yupislyr.

9:27 a.m.: "I'm not normally a praying man. But I'm

praying right now."—ColdChef.

For those who experienced or witnessed the events of September 11, 2001, it was a day that changed the world. People had a sense that 20 or even 100 years from now, we would look back on this event as one that fundamentally altered the way we look at the world, an event of epic proportions such as Pearl Harbor, the Protestant Reformation, or the Russian Revolution. It has left us a world that is less predictable than its predecessor. We can never again feel as secure as we felt at the dawn of that day. The world is at war, but it's a war unlike any other in history.

September 11 may have had its greatest impact in the economic arena. For months afterward markets would rally frantically on the barest hint of good news, only to sink just as rapidly at harbingers of further disruption. *Crain's Chicago Business*, in a special issue about September 11, described the dramatic changes that have also taken place in the world of business. "If anything, the terrorist attacks were the ugly finale to a gilded age for business. In their wake it's clear that the drivers of the great bull market of the 1990s—profits and productivity—must now take a back seat to people, security, and . . . armed conflict."

In the United States the changes involved were more than just military, political, and economic, although those certainly took center stage after September 11. We have seen profound differences in the way individuals approach life. There has been a rebirth of patriotism, something not seen on this scale since World War II. While remaining suspicious of religion, many, like "ColdChef" above, began exploring the spiritual dimension for the first time in their lives. Three themes seem to be moving to the center of our consciousness: family, meaning, and making a difference in the world.

Angela Calman, a recent graduate of Harvard's John F.

Kennedy School of Government, was being courted by a high-profile public relations firm when September 11 rolled around. In the days after the attack, however, she decided to interview for a job as chief communications officer at the Cleveland Clinic Foundation. "My priorities changed," she said. "I realized I wanted to do something that matters. 9/11 was the catalyst for a major life change. I guess I found something I didn't even realize I was missing."

Angela Yoo took communication in college, signed up for internships, and finally received the offer of her dream job with *InStyle* magazine in New York. But on September 11 she realized that she no longer wanted what she had earned. The terrorist attacks left her longing to do something to help others. So in spite of six years of effort to earn the writing and reporting job, she quit to join a non-profit volunteer organization called New York Cares. If it were not for the events of September 11, "I wouldn't have had the courage or reason to do this," Yoo said. "I realized I wanted to help society or the city. Now I feel like I'm making a difference."

While many New Yorkers became more community oriented after September 11, others decided to find community somewhere else—anywhere else. For example, Michael Niewodowski made an instant decision to leave the New York area. A chef at the Windows on the World restaurant on the 107th floor of the north tower of the World Trade Center, he missed the attack by just one hour (several friends and coworkers died). After hearing the news, Niewodowski simply left all his belongings in his apartment, got into his car, and drove to Bradenton, Florida, to be with his family. He has returned to New York City only as a tourist, taking a few hours to gaze at ground zero, the site where he once worked. "My priorities have been rearranged," he says. "Before, my career was my first priority. Now it's my family. I don't think I'll ever live in a big city again."

September 11 had the opposite effect on Don James and Mark Regazzi. Both are professors of religion at Andrews University, a small rural institution in the Midwest. Although in his 50s, James had never visited New York City. Within two weeks of the event he felt a "call" to go to New York City, find a high-rise apartment, and walk the streets, meeting, greeting, and encouraging people. When people asked what he was doing in New York, he simply said, "I came to help. I just feel that people in New York City need encouragement right now." The response was positive. Although not "big-city types," Don and his wife, Ruth, fell in love with New York City and hope to return as often as their lives in the Midwest allow.

Regazzi and his wife, on the other hand, grew up in New York City. The couple decided it was time to return to their roots. Renting a midtown apartment, they held parties, inviting old high school friends, residents of their building, and even people they met on the street and in cafés. They found New Yorkers to be warm and accepting people who valued their attempts to build community in the big city. Although Regazzi had to return after a couple months to take up his classes at the university once more, the experience rekindled the couple's youthful love affair with New York. "We have decided to buy an apartment somewhere in Manhattan, return as often as we can, and eventually retire there," Lydie Regazzi told me. "We don't want ever to turn our back on these relationships."

September 11 was a day that changed the world. In this book we will explore some of the transformations in the military, political, and economic landscape, and discover the role the Internet played in them. At times we will peer into the murky glass of an uncertain future, trying to make sense of it all. To do that, we will explore America's frantic attempts to defend itself through high-tech weapons, electronic eavesdropping, and a renewed interest in the dirty side of spying. We will strive to understand the interplay between Christianity and Islam that seems to lie behind these events, especially by exploring the anatomy of a terrorist; the forces and ideas that could turn a mama's boy into a mass murderer in a few short years. In addition, we will also seek to understand the realities that drove Osama bin Laden into his hatred of America and its philosophy of life.

The Purpose of This Book

Above all else, we will examine the spiritual implications of this event and the changes it introduced into our world. September 11 altered the way millions of people viewed God and their relationship to Him. Many believers found themselves confused by His seeming absence in the face of enormous tragedy and pain. Yet many more, believers and unbelievers alike, discovered tokens of His presence in the midst of the disaster. People began to find time for God in a world that seemed to have gone mad.

I am not talking about a rebirth of "religion" here. September 11 did not lessen suspicion of religion. If anything, the terrorist links to Islamic fundamentalism and the conservative Christian calls for revenge raised fresh questions about the role of religion in building a just and peaceful society. At the same time, however, these events have highlighted the need for a Higher Power and purpose for life. Any spiritual organization that wishes to meet that need, however, must take a careful look at its own motives and practices first. As with Judaism after the Holocaust, spiritual business as usual no longer seems appropriate. Flip and shallow answers are no longer welcome.

One more thing. I realize the peril of trying to put how

I feel about September 11 into words. A New Yorker named Dan Fahrbach spoke at a memorial service a few days later. As I remember it, he said something like "We have used up all our big words on relatively small things. At a time like September 11 silence is unbearable, but speech is even worse. What happened cannot be described in words. But many people are discovering that there are words from long ago that speak for us. The pages of the Bible contain words that express the inexpressible. There are stories and sayings that draw out meaning at times and in places where no meaning seemed possible."

In a world where shallow and confident answers have become suspect, the Bible is not afraid to ask the hard questions and explore dueling answers. Scripture portrays a God who is pleased when people care enough to shake their fist at Him. He is a God who faced the agonizing death of His Son with purposeful silence. Such a God may be hard to understand, but He is never boring (even though some who worship Him may be). He may be hard to find at times, but when we do find Him, He is worth the time we spent seeking Him. From my quest for God to yours, this book is about an experience that has never been more relevant than it is today, in the aftermath of September 11.

SOURCES

Armour, Stephanie. "After September 11, Some Workers Turn Lives Upside Down." *USA Today,* May 8, 2002.

Cauchon, Dennis. "For Many on Sept. 11, Survival Was No Accident." *USA Today,* Dec. 19, 2001.

Crain's Chicago Business, special issue about September 11, 2001.

William Johnsson. "Ash Tuesday." *Adventist Review,* Jan. 3, 2002, pp. 16-20.

Yahoo! Internet Life, November 2001, pp. 77, 79.

2

THE ISLAMIC WORLD OF
OSAMA BIN LADEN

The instigators of the attack on the World Trade Center intended it as a blow against the United States and its Christian heritage. The results of that attack, however, were not limited to the target. The roll of those who died at ground zero included people from literally scores of nations and faith convictions. The targeting of innocents makes no distinction between friends and enemies, between fellow believers and those who differ, a point illustrated by a rescue that took place just before the twin towers collapsed.

Usman Farman is a Pakistani Muslim who worked on the twenty-seventh floor of one of the trade towers on September 11. As he left the tower he fell stunned to the ground, perhaps as a result of flying debris. When a Hasidic Jew found Farman lying on the ground he did not hesitate. "He helped me stand up," Farman reported, "and we ran for what seemed like forever without looking back. He was the last person I would ever have thought would help me. If it weren't for him I probably would have been engulfed in shattered glass and debris." Did the terrorist attackers realize that scores of faithful Muslims such as Farman would die that day, along with many others who had nothing to do with American policy? The suffering of the survivors cuts across many lines of faith.

Michael Baksh, a Pakistani Christian, had been without a job for a while. September 11 was his first day of work on the ninety-fourth floor of the World Trade Center. His wife and two young children said goodbye that morning not knowing that he would never return. To make matters even worse, his remains have never been found. So in the days after the September 11 attack, his wife, Christina, felt the need to establish a special place where she, her son, and her 7-year-old daughter could remember Michael. She purchased a cemetery plot and held a service on October 5 over a tiny hole in the ground.

"This small space in the ground seemed so unrepresentative of a man's life," said the family pastor, Samir Selmanovic, of the Church of the Advent of Hope. Without a body to bury, Baksh's family and friends dropped reminders of him into a hole—a favorite Knicks T-shirt, photos, a plastic bone from the family's cocker spaniel. Baksh's 2-year-old son, James, added a plastic golf ball—a gift from Dad. Selmanovic added his own contribution to the memorabilia placed in the hole: a page torn from his Bible, containing a promise of future resurrection.

Shortly after the "burial," his relatives and those of other victims had something else with which to remember their loved ones: chalky gray ash recovered from ground zero. Each victim's family received an urn filled with contents from the collapsed towers—soil, ash, or dirt—to serve as a remembrance. But for many families, the containers only added to their confusion over how to obtain closure. How long should they wait for the authorities to identify body parts? What if searchers found remains after family and friends had held a memorial? Above all, what do you do with burial ash that represents the lives of thousands?

Baksh's wife, Christina, decided to go back and bury the ash-filled urn with the other items. "There is so much sadness wrapped up in that urn," she said. "Yet my husband loved New York so much, and now in a way, he is one with New York City."

The struggle over how to say goodbye without a body

19

present was a challenge that reverberated across metropolitan New York in churches, mosques, temples, and Buddhist funeral halls, where ancient traditions had to be altered according to the circumstance. For Abul Chowdhury's family, that meant no ritual washing of the body, no prayers offered over a body wrapped in white and placed toward Mecca in a traditional Muslim ceremony. At his memorial mourners, who included many non-Muslims from Chowdhury's firm, Cantor Fitzgerald, offered prayers and listened as the Talgheen—a reminder of the deceased's beliefs—was recited. Chowdhury's sister, Zubaida Rahman, longed for some tangible evidence of his demise. "I am praying hard for something, even a finger, to bury in the cemetery," she said. "But because Muslim law says prayers must be offered within 40 days of death for the soul to be at peace, I convinced my mother and father and his wife to go ahead with the memorial."

One Jewish family has had to return to the cemetery several times as additional body parts turned up, because Jewish custom is to bury all parts found. In the Hindu faith, on the other hand, cremation is the traditional burial rite. Uma Mysorekar, president of the Hindu Temple Society of North America, said: "It is hard for the families to accept the idea that the remains of thousands along with building debris is what can be scattered in substitute of pure remains. But I believe the families will come to accept this view. The Hindu faith says we are all one, and that is the way it is."

Family and friends of Doris Eng, a manager at the Windows on the World restaurant in the World Trade Center, gathered at the China Buddhist Association in Flushing, New York, where brown-robed nuns tapped time with hollowed wooden "fish" and chanted to an altar dedicated to Eng. "With a body, we would offer chants and prayers to an open casket in the temple, not before an altar in this funeral hall," Eng's brother, Jerry, explained. Without tangible remains, Eng placed a nameplate honoring his sister, who had just celebrated her thirtieth birthday, in the funeral hall. Because of the importance of sending the soul to the next life as quickly as possible, Eng's family decided not to wait for the urns to arrive.

Did the terrorists care that in taking down the World Trade Center towers they were killing hundreds of people from nearly half the nations in the world? Did they have no discrimination at all in their hatred? Was Osama bin Laden simply a mass murderer without a conscience? Did he somehow find joy in the slaughter of innocents?

Many place the blame squarely on Osama bin Laden's religion, Islam. Note the strong words of archconservative commentator Ann Coulter: "Airports scrupulously apply the same laughably ineffective airport harassment to Suzy Chapstick as to Muslim hijackers. It is preposterous to assume every passenger is a potential crazed homicidal maniac. We know who the homicidal maniacs are. They are the ones cheering and dancing right now. We should invade their countries, kill their leaders and convert them to Christianity. We weren't punctilious about locating and punishing only Hitler and his top officers. We carpet-bombed German cities: we killed civilians. That's war. And this is war" (in *Yahoo! Internet Life,* November 2001, p. 77).

Such a judgment is blatantly unfair. It doesn't take a rocket scientist to figure out that terrorism does not restrict itself to Muslims and Islamic organizations. The list of twentieth-century terrorists includes the Irish Republican Army, the Jews who blew up the King David Hotel in 1946, Puerto Rican nationalists, Basque separatists, the Shining Path guerrilla movement of Peru, Tamil separatists in Sri Lanka, the Italian Red Brigades, the Baader-Meinhof Gang in Germany, the Croatian separatists of the former Yugoslavia, and the Japanese Red Army. To my knowledge, none of the above involved any Muslims. And even a short visit to the Middle East makes it clear that the vast majority of Muslims are not terrorists either. Nevertheless, the tie between Islam and terrorism seems particularly acute after September 11, and it is worth some effort to understand the reasons for it.

A Middle Eastern Perspective

Ann Coulter's attitude strikes me as the reaction of someone viewing the Middle East from a distance. In order to understand Osama bin Laden, it helps to have spent some time in the region and to have some appreciation of the role of Islam in Middle Eastern life and experience. I made my first trip to the Middle East in 1995. My family and I went through a detailed strip search before boarding the last leg of our flight in Frankfurt, Germany. We landed near Tel Aviv in the late afternoon and entered Jerusalem after dark. Somewhat reluctantly, the Israeli driver agreed to drop us off in front of a guest center in East Jerusalem, a few hundred yards from the center of Arab life in that ancient city.

After a quick snack of hummus, fresh veggies, and pita bread, we wearily threw coverings on our beds and fell asleep, jet-lagged from the 22-hour overnight trip. No one moved for more than three hours. But around 1:30 in the morning we all came awake one by one. My 9-year-old son, in particular, was so hyped that he began a running commentary on what was going through his mind.

"Do you see the shadows in the room?"

"Quiet, Joel," I said.

"OK, but the ones over your head look like a church window."

"That's nice, Joel, but I'm trying to sleep. Please be quiet."

Silence for two minutes. Then: "I think there's somebody outside the window."

That got my attention. After all, we were in the land of suicide bombers. I stretched up in my top bunk and looked carefully out the window, but saw and heard nothing. "Get to sleep, Joel. There's no one out there."

"I can't sleep."

"Neither can I, but we've got to try. Now, not another word, do you hear me?"

"Yes, Daddy, but wait a minute. What was that brown stuff you ate on the plane?"

"Joel, I don't want to talk about that right now! I want to sleep! You're keeping everyone awake. Just lie still and close your eyes."

"I tried that and it didn't work . . ."

So it went for the better part of three hours. First one child, then another (I have three), vented their frustration at being unable to sleep. Jet lag is no fun, no matter how exciting the place you have traveled to. Then at 4:17 a.m. (I will never forget the time—I looked at my watch) I heard the strangest sound of my life—a melodious voice coming over a loudspeaker, singing in a mournful style, somewhat reminiscent of medieval monks. Barely had that voice begun when it was joined by another, then many more. Each came from a different location, each singing a different tune, all blending into a haunting cacophony of sound that gripped me in the pit of my soul. Suddenly I was the one who couldn't resist talking.

"Do you all hear that?"

"Weird," one kid commented.

"Cool," another said.

"What is it?" the third asked.

"It's the Muslim call to prayer," I explained. "They do it five times a day. I guess one of those times is at 4:00 in the morning."

"Why can't they talk English?"

"This is the Middle East. They speak Arabic here. Now you *know* how far you have come." Perhaps the Muslim call to prayer has a soothing effect. The sounds died away within 10 minutes and, amazingly, we all fell asleep for three more hours. But that early-morning call to prayer defined our transition from the United States to the Middle East. There is nothing in the world quite like it. You *know* you are in the Middle East when you hear those haunting sounds on every side. We were in the land of Abraham, Moses, and Muhammad.

The next morning we set out to explore our new neighborhood. An eight-foot-high wall topped with broken glass surrounded the compound of the guest center. We passed through the door and went out into the street. After about 100 yards we encountered a lot of foot traffic. Men and women dressed in flowing robes and head coverings. The head covering of the men was the kaffiyeh, well known in the West from the one Yasser Arafat wears wherever he goes. The women had on kerchiefs like those of older Eastern European women. Such costumes in a setting of run-down stone buildings made it feel as if we were back in ancient times.

Soon we were passing through the Damascus Gate into the old city of Jerusalem. The pounding beat of modern Arab music welcomed us to the crowded marketplace, where shoppers could bargain for clothing, spices, candy, falafels, baklava, music, and household appliances. I kept careful tabs on my wallet as we rubbed shoulders with the locals in the crowded alleys of the souk, the Arab marketplace. Nothing in all my 45 years of life could have prepared me for both the strangeness and the delight of that experience.

My family and I stayed in Palestinian Jerusalem for 10

weeks. We ate Arab food and became friends with many. I think of Marwan, the shopkeeper, who always took time to talk about current events and give me advice on how to behave in an Arab community. Gabriel, the travel agent, had his ear to the Palestinian underground and was careful to send us places only when it was safe to do so. I remember the nameless falafel vendor I rescued one day when an errant vehicle knocked over his stand. His gratitude was overwhelming. To this day he immediately recognizes me and greets me with a hug and a kiss, no matter how long I have been away.

My time in the Middle East (I have also been to Egypt three times, to Turkey twice, and to Jordan once) has been most meaningful. The region has become part of me now. As a New Yorker I have deep sympathy for the sufferings of the Jews. I am glad that they have a homeland that they can call their own. At the same time, my heart goes out to the Palestinian people who share that land with them. I saw Israeli soldiers, often looking no older than 16, carrying machine guns with an air of authority. They challenged Palestinian youths and shopkeepers, yelling at them and prodding them with their weapons. I sensed the Palestinian helplessness. Occasionally they shared their frustration and rage with me.

The *salem* in Jerusalem means "peace," but Jerusalem is a very angry city. One notices a lot of shouting, pushing, and shoving going on, and not just between Israeli and Arab, or Christian and Muslim, but among Muslims and Christians themselves. In the Old City the powder is dry and the fuse is short. My falafel friend almost came to blows one day over some dispute or other. I stopped walking and hung around, in case he needed help, but after a few minutes things quieted down. Another time I watched Orthodox Jews march through the Arab section, shoving

Arabs aside if they got in the way, secure in the knowledge that soldiers up on the walls would take care of things if anyone protested. A couple times the Palestinians mistook me for an Israeli. The first time a Coke bottle glanced off my shoulder and shattered at my feet. A laughing child, no more than 7 years old, had dropped it from a bridge. Another time stones thrown by three boys no more than 10 barely missed me.

It surprised me when I learned the obvious differences between Muslims and Christians in Arab Jerusalem. When you go into a grocery store and see alcohol, you know that the owner is a Christian. A Muslim grocery owner would not sell alcohol. An Arab woman dressed like a European is a Christian, because a Muslim would wear far more modest clothing. Since most Israelis would line up with the Christians on these two points, I began to see how Muslims could come to view Christians and Jews as holding to an inferior faith. If, on top of that, Israelis act like oppressors and the Christian West does nothing about it, it paints Judeo-Christianity with the same stroke.

It is for reasons such as this that I sense some reserve toward Americans in the Middle East. On my first visit to Egypt we traveled by boat from the port of Aqaba in Jordan to the Egyptian port of Nuweiba on the Sinai coast. The ship's crew directed all Americans to the first-class lounge, an air-conditioned hall in the center of the ferry that had TVs, drinks, and luxurious accommodations. But as we looked out the windows at the coastline of Saudi Arabia passing in the midday heat, it dawned on me that I saw no locals anywhere in sight. So I decided to go exploring through the ship. I discovered hundreds of Arabs scattered across the top deck in the hot sun, sitting on metal bulkheads and extended benches. Some were trying to sleep right on the metal deck. Many were wearing dirty or tattered clothing. Clearly it was not the wealthy section of the ship.

A young Saudi, sitting in a bit of shade on the bench along the side of the ship, noticed the American walking around and called to me in excellent English. He was very polite, but he jumped at the chance to open up some political issues. His view of the world was very different from mine, yet compelling in its own way. He shared his sense that the American government wanted to be seen as beneficent, yet based its actions and demands on self-interest. Arab people like the freedom and openness of American society, but they don't like its immorality and "big stick" attitude toward other countries. Finally he put his frustration in direct terms: "Why does everything always have to go America's way?" It was a new way of looking at things for me. Until then, I had thought of Middle Eastern countries as the ones who were unreasonable and demanding.

In 1999 I made my second visit to Egypt. This time I was able to get away from the hotel and tourist circuit to spend a few days in an urban "village" of about 50,000 people, an hour's drive outside of Cairo. Every evening a couple English-speaking Egyptian friends would take me for walks through the village, usually stopping at a shop that sold cookies, candy, and ice cream. As the days went by I struck up a friendship with the shopkeeper, who looked forward to our evening visits. At that time NATO forces were entering Kosovo to protect the Muslim majority there from the atrocities raging under the name of ethnic cleansing. The shopkeeper had an Arabic newspaper open to news of the conflict.

I wondered if the action in Kosovo might have changed some Arab minds about the United States and its goals in the world. So I asked the shopkeeper, through my friends, what he thought of the bombing of Serbia and the occupation of Kosovo. He smiled ruefully, took a puff on a cigarette, shook his head, and said, "Do you want to know my real opinion?"

"Yes," I replied.

"I think this is Monica's war," he grinned. "This is the way the American president diverts attention from himself." I would have been more disappointed if I hadn't been aware that many Americans had been saying the same thing!

A couple years later I was getting off a plane with friends in Luxor, Egypt. A travel agent met us in baggage claim and gave us some instructions for the day. He then asked one of my friends what he did for a living. The man said he worked for a Christian church. The agent's eyes immediately brightened. "Then you are rich!" he exclaimed. His comment served as a summary of many Egyptian attitudes toward the Christian West. They see it as a different kind of world—uncaring, greedy, and rich. It is useful to have Westerners around, but one should never take their beliefs seriously.

A Bigger Picture

During the Middle Ages Muslim governments were generally more tolerant of other faiths than were the Christian governments of Europe. But that was not always the case. For example, when Muhammad was born Christian communities flourished all over North Africa. They produced such famous Christians such as Tertullian, Cyprian, Athanasius, and Augustine. But after the Muslim conquests began in the seventh century the invaders discriminated against Christians with special taxes and social disapproval. As a result, Christianity gradually dwindled away in North Africa and is virtually absent now except in Egypt, where, according to the CIA, Christians make up about *9* percent of the population.

Both suppression of other faiths and tolerance for them

has roots in the Muslim holy book, the Qur'an. On the one hand, it encourages Muslims to avoid compulsion in religion (2:256). Jews and Christians are "nearest in affection" and are to be allowed to practice their faith as long as they perform their obligations as loyal citizens (5:82). The Qur'an summons Muslims to "invite (all) to the way of your Lord with wisdom and beautiful preaching; and argue with them in ways that are best and most gracious: for your Lord knows best who has strayed from His Path, and who receives guidance" (16:125).

On the other hand, many commands in the Qur'an encourage warfare, especially when regarded as defensive in nature (2:190-192; 47:1-4): "Fight in the cause of God those who fight you . . . and slay them." "Tumult and oppression are worse than slaughter." "When you meet those who disbelieve, smite the necks." According to the Qur'an, those who resist Islam "shall be put to death or crucified or have their hands and feet cut off on alternate sides" (5:51). While Christians and Jews should receive special consideration, Muslims must not show any mercy to "infidels" (9:5). So when terrorists like Bin Laden use such terms as *Infidel America*, they are expressing the belief that destroying American innocents and property pleases God.

How does one move from the Qur'an's justification of defensive war to the slaughter of large numbers of innocents in the name of religion? Here we must probe deeply into the terrorist mentality. Islamic terrorists do not see themselves as undermining the clear teachings of Islam. Rather they believe that they are the true interpreters of the Qur'an and the traditions. They have come to believe, in fact, that the attacks on September 11 were "defensive actions," because Islam itself has come under attack from America, requiring defensive measures. To understand this mentality even a little, we must talk about the Qur'anic concept of jihad, or holy war.

Terrorist groups have long called themselves names such as "Islamic Jihad." In 1998 Osama bin Laden urged a "jihad against Crusaders and Jews" to justify the bombing of the U.S. embassies in Africa. For him such jihad justified any Muslim "to kill the Americans and plunder their money wherever and whenever they are found." But within Islam jihad is not a clear-cut concept. It does not merely describe military warfare in defense of the faith. A better translation for *jihad* might actually be "effort" or "struggle" (the Qur'an contains other words for "war" and "fighting"). Often it describes not warfare, but the personal struggle to be a better person, a better Muslim. However one translates it, jihad is a powerful concept in the Muslim world. When justified by the course of events, it becomes a personal obligation that stands above all others.

The Grievances of Osama bin Laden

Osama bin Laden's call for jihad rested on the conviction that Americans have declared war "on God, his messenger and Muslims." In other words, America and Americans have committed "crimes against Islam." How could he possibly have come to such a conclusion? It involves several factors. (As I write, it remains uncertain whether Bin Laden is alive or dead. I will speak of him and his ideas in the past tense only for convenience.)

The first of them is the Israeli-Palestinian situation. The history behind it looks very different to Arab eyes. While securing a homeland for Jews made a lot of sense in the West after the Holocaust, the original partition of Palestine came at the expense of Arabs whose ancestors had been in the land for centuries. The British had promised, during World War I, to support Arab independence in exchange for Arab aid against the Turks (remember the movie *Lawrence of Arabia?*). Then during World War II President Roosevelt promised at least one Arab leader that the major powers would not do anything about Palestine after the war without consulting the Arabs first.

Nevertheless, worldwide sympathy for the plight of the Jews during the war resulted in a United Nations partition that ceded more than half of Palestine to the Jews, although only a third of the population was Jewish and Jews owned an even smaller percentage of the land. In subsequent fighting the Israelis gained control of the entire land and continue building settlements in the West Bank and Gaza despite UN resolutions requiring the return of land conquered in 1967. To Arab eyes this looks suspiciously like a revival of the Crusades of the Middle Ages, with Israel at the forefront and America guiding behind the scenes.

I do not want the reader to misunderstand me here. I know that the Israeli perspective would tell the story quite differently. But I think it is important for our purpose to see through the eyes of the terrorist, as far as that is possible for us to do. Jewish desperation after the Holocaust was real, and for many Jews the homeland in the Middle East was the only spark of hope at the time. But the desperation of the Palestinian refugee camps remains to this day. People living in perpetual poverty are dying at the expense of weapons purchased with the billions of dollars in military aid America gives Israel each year. From the Muslim viewpoint this is a serious and ongoing injustice that has never been addressed. For Bin Laden the situation was criminal.

A second major grievance of Bin Laden had to do with the corrupt and secular governments ruling most Muslim countries. He viewed the governments of such countries as Egypt, Jordan, Saudi Arabia, and Iraq as unelected, oppressive, pandering to the West, and soft on

Islam. It is not surprising that Bin Laden, himself a Saudi, soon became unwelcome in Saudi Arabia. Its government viewed him as a greater threat to the sheiks of Saudi Arabia than he was to the United States. He believed that secular Arab leaders are mere tools of the West, using the power of the West to cement their own personal position at the expense of the Muslim masses. While the United States did not set up these governments directly, in the minds of Islamic extremists they would not survive without American support.

A third major grievance concerns the physical presence of the American military in Saudi Arabia since 1990. For many Muslims, the holiness of Mecca and Medina extends over the entire nation. This has been perhaps the crucial issue for Bin Laden. In the 1980s he was not hostile to America despite the Israeli-Palestinian situation. Evidence suggests that he may have been on the CIA payroll for a time. But while he opposed the aggression of Saddam Hussein in Kuwait, he was distressed and then infuriated by the decision of the Saudi government to invite the Americans and other Westerners to "occupy" the Holy Land. The alcoholism, materialism, immorality, and relative nudity exhibited by Western troops in Saudi Arabia seem sacrilegious to many moderate Muslims. To Bin Laden they bordered on blasphemy.

While it is not as vital to the big picture as the first three factors, Bin Laden seems to have felt betrayed by the Americans in Afghanistan. When the Russians invaded Afghanistan in 1979 he led a band of mujahedin seeking to drive the Soviets out. America had an interest in assisting any forces willing to fight the Russians. That support made Americans the good guys through the 1980s. But in 1989 the Russians left Afghanistan and the Americans immediately lost interest, abandoning Bin Laden and his mujahedin to their own devices. Afghanistan disintegrated into a multitude of factions. Thus Bin Laden felt betrayed.

A final grievance of Bin Laden has been more general. Historically through the centuries Muslims have often had the upper hand politically and militarily. For at least 1,000 years the Islamic Empire and its Turkish successor were superpowers. But during the past couple hundred years the Western powers divided up the Muslim world among themselves. Since that time the Muslim region has been a backwater in world affairs. Were it not for the fact that much of the world's oil supply comes from the Middle East, the major powers might pay it no attention at all.

In a Western-dominated world Muslims feel humiliated on every side. The Israelis (Palestine and the regional wars of 1956, 1967, and 1973), the Serbs (in Bosnia and Kosovo), the Russians (in Chechnya and other Muslim republics of central Asia), and the Indians (in Kashmir and various parts of India) have all found ways to marginalize Muslim interests around the world. On top of these slights the West has "imposed" Western law codes on Muslim states, enforced Western economic ideas, including the charging of interest (contrary to Islamic law), and exported alcohol, drugs, pornography, and crime. It frustrates many devout Muslims when they believe that the Islamic culture is superior, yet find themselves forced to acknowledge that America has vastly superior power and wealth.

Bin Laden's Strategy for September 11

For Bin Laden the crucial question became how to restore Islam to a dominant place in the world again. Could diplomacy accomplish that? Experience told him that it would not work. The West had been "negotiating" with the Middle East for more than a century, and what was the result? The establishment of Israel, for one thing. Another consequence was the colonial powers dividing the Middle East into artificial nations with no consideration of tribal territories and local interests. Meanwhile the West grew richer and more powerful, and the Muslim world became increasingly irrelevant.

Should the Muslim world stand up and fight in military terms then? In its present state of weakness that would be foolish. Anyone unconvinced by the dominance of the Israeli attacks in 1967 and 1982 (in Lebanon) should have no further doubts about the West's strength after the Gulf War and the recent conflict in Afghanistan. In an age of information technology both the American and Israeli military are overwhelming and incontestable. Any form of direct frontal assault would be the equivalent of suicide. So for Bin Laden, there remained only one alternative to helplessness, and that was terrorism.

This gives us some insight into the mind-set of Bin Laden when he gave the go-ahead for the attack of September 11, 2001. While the actions of the highjackers were gruesome and incomprehensible to Westerners, they are part of a strategic plan to change the balance of power in the world. The leaders of al-Qaeda see the Islamic world being occupied by non-Islamic forces. To alter the situation al-Qaeda must find a way to end the "occupation" and reunite Islam. Since the United States is the leading power in the world and the patron of many Islamic regimes, it has become the great enemy that motivates and controls an anti-Islamic agenda.

Defeating the United States is not a realistic option. But the kind of terrorism Bin Laden has unleashed does burden America with billions of dollars of expenses to fight terrorism at home and abroad. It distracts Americans with the constant fear of unexpected attacks. Rendering Americans as insecure as Europeans and Israelis have felt for decades, it makes isolationism look more attractive. If, in the process, terrorism can cause the United States to withdraw from the Islamic world, other anti-Islamic powers such as Russia, China, and Israel would be helpless to intervene. Corrupt and secular governments in the Muslim world would then have no base of outside support, and the Islamic masses could overthrow them.

So it is unlikely that al-Qaeda expects to destroy the United States directly. It is too powerful and too distant for that to happen. Rather, Bin Laden's strategy seems to be to force the United States into a series of actions that destabilize the governments of those Middle Eastern countries that depend on Washington for their survival. If pressure from the United States forces those governments to join the U.S. in fighting Islamic militants or to remain silent in the face of Israeli aggression, popular uprisings could easily lead to their collapse. The ultimate goal would be the establishment of an Islamic superpower, a vast Islamic state stretching from Morocco to the island of Mindanao in the Philippines, all governed by Islamic law.

Could Bin Laden achieve such goals? He clearly believed the United States does not have the stomach to suppress a massive and popular uprising. Unlike al-Qaeda, Americans as a rule do their best not to hurt innocents. The same military that is virtually invincible in battle would have a difficult time handling an army of unarmed women and children. Although the United States has important interests in the Islamic world, they are not on a scale to justify the expense and casualties involved in a long-term occupation. To the degree that further terrorist acts in the U.S. should occur, the American populace could easily swing toward an isolationist stance. If such isolationism should lead to withdrawal from Afghanistan and Saudi Arabia and even the partial abandonment of Israel, the political world would have changed considerably in favor of the Islamic agenda.

So from Bin Laden's perspective, war in diplomatic, economic, or military terms would result only in the further humiliation of Islam. But terrorism has altered the battle-field odds. Since the targets vastly outnumber the defend-ers, al-Qaeda has designed a war strategy in which it has significant advantages. It weakens American power in that the United States must spread its defensive measures over a wide area. Suicidal fervor creates a low-tech battlefield that neutralizes superior technology. Will all or part of Bin Laden's grand design succeed? Whether or not he is alive today, the battle is far from over. September 11 continues to be a day that changed the world.

SOURCES

Bacchiocchi, Samuele. "Reflection on Terrorism." *End Time Issues Newsletter,* no. 75, e-mailed on October 16, 2001, from sbacchiocchi@qtm.net.

Central Intelligence Agency Web site at www.cia.gov.

"The Day That Changed America." *Newsweek,* Dec. 31, 2001/Jan. 7, 2002, pp. 40-71.

Donner, Fred M. "The Sources of Islamic Conceptions of War," in *Just War and Jihad: Historical and Theoretical Perspectives on War and Peace in Western and Islamic Traditions.* Ed. John Kelsay and James Turner Johnson. New York: Greenwood Press, 1991.

Firestone, Reuven. *JIHÂD: The Origin of Holy War in Islam.* New York: Oxford University Press, 1999.

"Jewish Group to Start Armed Patrols in Brooklyn." *USA Today,* June 10, 2002.

Koran, The. Trans. from the Arabic by J. M. Rodwell. Intro. by G. Margoliouth. Everyman's Library. London: J. M. Dent and Sons, 1909.

Mayer, Ann Elizabeth. "War and Peace in the Islamic Tradition and International Law," in *Just War and Jihad: Historical and Theoretical Perspectives on War and Peace in Western and Islamic Traditions.* Ed. John Kelsay and James Turner Johnson. New York: Greenwood Press, 1991.

Mallouhi, Christine A. *Waging Peace on Islam.* Downer's Grove, Ill.: InterVarsity Press, 2000.

Premium Global Intelligence briefings posted at stratfor.com.

Swartley, Willard. *Slavery, Sabbath, War and Women: Case Issues in Biblical Interpretation.* Scottdale, Pa.: Herald Press, 1983.

Woodberry, J. Dudley. "The War on Terrorism: Reflections of a Guest in the Lands Involved."

Woodbury, Margaret A. "With Bodies Lost in Rubble, Mourners Forgo Traditional Rites," San Francisco *Chronicle,* Oct. 14, 2001.

Woodward, Kenneth L. "The Bible and the Qur'an: Searching the Holy Books for Roots of Conflict and Seeds of Reconciliation." *Newsweek,* Feb. 11, 2002, pp. 51-57.

———. "How Should We Think About Islam?" *Newsweek,* Dec. 31, 2001/Jan. 7, 2002, pp. 102, 105.

Yahoo! Internet Life, November 2001, pp. 77, 89.

3
ANATOMY OF A TERRORIST

Except for the place where they died, Bill Feehan and Mohamed Atta would seem to have had absolutely nothing in common. . . . As a lifelong firefighter who rose to become first deputy commissioner of the New York City Fire Department, Feehan was directly or indirectly responsible for saving thousands of lives. As a suicidal terrorist who flew American Airlines Flight 11 into the north tower of the World Trade Center, Atta murdered thousands, including Bill Feehan, who was helping a woman at the base of the north tower when the building collapsed on him. Any suggestion of moral equivalence between the two men is repugnant. And yet, it must be said, both believed in the rightness of their causes with absolute certainty" (in *Newsweek,* Dec. 31, 2001/Jan. 7, 2002, p. 40).

Is there an "anatomy of a terrorist"? How is it that two wiggly baby boys could one day end up in the same place but for such different reasons? And how could anyone come to accept the slaughter of innocents as the "right" thing to do? It would be a lot easier on most of us if we could believe that Mohamed Atta was totally insane, the victim of mad delusions. But could a truly crazy person work with the calm and careful purpose that he exhibited? Does it make more sense to assume that he was simply evil? And if so, how did he get that way?

According to a description in *Newsweek*, based on interviews with family and others who knew him, Mohamed Atta would have seemed an unlikely candidate for terrorist action. Short and slim (in the highjacking of

American Airlines Flight 11 he was leader and pilot while the other four highjackers provided the brawn), he was considered a "mama's boy" by his father. Atta Senior would complain to his wife that she was raising Mohamed as a girl. Even in his 20s the younger Atta continued to sit in his mother's lap from time to time. As a further problem for a prospective highjacker, he absolutely hated flying! His sister, who was a doctor, had to provide him medicine for cramps and vomiting every time he flew.

An interesting obsession of his, however, offered a premonition of the shocking way that he would choose to die. On the wall of Mohamed Atta's apartment in Hamburg, Germany, hung a black-and-white poster of construction workers perched on a beam of the Empire State Building high above New York (taken back in 1930). According to his teachers and former classmates, Atta believed that high-rise buildings were a curse introduced into the Middle East from the West. In the Middle East the traditional method of construction has been one- or two-story houses with private courtyards. When done well, it results in the kind of charming, bustling neighborhood life that tourists to the Middle East love to taste. The interior courtyards provide privacy, the beauty of the neighborhood creates dignity, and the whole fosters interaction and community.

In the 1960s and 1970s, however, Middle Eastern cities and towns became filled with impersonal and ugly apartment complexes. Atta's own family moved into an eleventh-floor apartment in 1990, just as he was graduating with an engineering degree from Cairo University. The building his own family lived in became for him a shabby symbol of Egypt's embrace of Western ways. Secular Arabs had accepted the negative trappings of the modern world without attaining its wealth and freedom.

Atta began to study ways to reverse the situation and

restore the old glories of Islam. A major opportunity came when his father decided to send him to engineering school at Hamburg Technical University in Germany. There he pursued a degree in urban-planning studies. His thesis focused on the restoration of Aleppo, an ancient Syrian city, to its pure Islamic past—devoid of skyscrapers. He received a B+ for the thesis.

But how did the mama's boy become a mass murderer? Atta's progress from idealistic student to Islamic militant to terrorist seems to have been gradual. At first his goal was the improvement of urban life in the Middle East. Then in Cairo University he came under the influence of the Muslim Brotherhood, a movement that sought to create an Islamic state and limit Western influence in Egypt through nonviolent means.

The anti-foreigner attitude in Germany, which often made Muslim immigrants feel like second-class citizens, probably sharpened Mohamed Atta's gathering resentments. He found refuge in the mosques of Hamburg, where the mullahs have a lot more freedom to speak than they do in Egypt. Recruiting for the terrorist underground sometimes occurs in these mosques. Investigators believe that Mohammed Haydar Zammar, a German citizen of Syrian descent, specifically recruited Atta into al-Qaeda.

In 1995 Atta went on a pilgrimage to Mecca, searching for a deeper commitment to his faith. Two years later he traveled to Afghanistan and enrolled in one of Osama bin Laden's training camps for terrorists. Egyptians received special treatment in the camps, so Atta would have quickly felt at home. The camps sought to solidify beliefs, fan the flames of hatred, and then train people for specialized roles in the mission of terror. The al-Qaeda chose Atta for a leadership role and trained him in the arts of bomb making and chemical weaponry. While he was not intimidating in appearance, he seems to have had a hard stare that made it difficult for people to cross him. Power is more than just a physical thing.

When he returned to Hamburg in 1998 he established an al-Qaeda cell that included two roommates, Marwan Al-Shehhi and Ziad Samir Jarrah, who also participated in the suicide highjackings on September 11. All three came from middle-class families, were skilled in computers, and were highly educated. Once set on his course, Atta made further preparation by getting flight training in Florida, examining potential targets in the U.S., and finally heading for Portland, Maine, where he was to board a connecting flight to Boston with one of his terrorist "musclemen," Abdulaziz Alomari. In Boston they were able to transfer without passing through further security, and the rest is history. A "mama's boy" who hated skyscrapers found a way to destroy one of the two most massive towers in the world, at the cost of thousands of human lives. And he did so in the name of God.

According to *Newsweek*, Mohamed Atta carefully planned out his final moves. In a document he titled "The Last Night," he wrote to himself: "Be happy, optimistic, calm, because you are heading for a deed God loves and will accept. It will be the day, God willing, you spend with the women of paradise." And with regard to the last moment before impact, Atta declared: "Either end your life while praying, seconds before the target, or make your last words: 'There is no God but God, Muhammad is His messenger.'" Was Atta's vision the inevitable product of Islam, or did he misunderstand the faith he served so fervently? Does the Qur'an itself contain the seeds of suicidal terrorism, or is al-Qaeda a blasphemous misinterpretation of Muhammad's original intentions?

The Qur'an and the Bible

Both the Bible and the Qur'an are in the format of books

of divine revelations. Between them they communicate the will of God for about half the world's population. Abraham and Moses appear as central figures in both books. The Qur'an even has positive portrayals of Jesus, although there are significant differences between the accounts of Jesus in the New Testament and those of the Qur'an. But although the two holy books have many elements in common, they differ in at least two fundamental ways.

One primary difference lies in the nature of the revelations themselves. The Bible reveals God through His progressive dealings in history. God meets people where they are. The Qur'an presents a very different picture. It does not offer segments of history or a coherent focus on any particular theme. Instead it reads like a stream of consciousness, jumping here and there from divine commands to stories of the ancients to theological pronouncements to prayers to a description of the final judgment. The Qur'an is not organized thought. It instead contains short recitations by Muhammad that others collected after his death and organized roughly from the longest to the shortest.

The style of the Qur'an, however, is grounded in its very nature. For Jews and Christians the Bible is the product of divinely inspired human beings, generally writing in their own words. Muslims, on the other hand, regard the Qur'an as the eternal words of Allah Himself. According to them, Muhammad played no role in shaping the recitations recorded in the Qur'an. They are the very words of God Himself spoken in the Arabic language, heard by Muhammad, and transcribed in Arabic by him. Thus the Qur'an is not the Bible of the Muslims, but rather functions for them more like Jesus Christ does for Christians. To quote Bob Woodward of *Newsweek:* "In short, if Christ is the word made flesh, the Qur'an is the word made book."

For the Muslim God is totally removed from human

contact (transcendent). So the closest any human being can possibly come to God in this life is in the text of the Qur'an. And since those words are the very words of Allah Himself, they are only truly valid in the original Arabic. Thus Muslims read the Qur'an and use it in prayers only in the Arabic language, even though the majority of Muslims do not understand it. But what counts for them is not the meaning and the content. The very sounds and syllables of the Arabic Qur'an mediate the presence of God to the one who reads and speaks them. So Islam is not primarily a doctrinal religion. With a few exceptions (there is no God but Allah and Muhammad is His messenger, for example), Islam is not about what a person believes so much as an experience of God resulting in obedience and submission to His will.

So the Qur'an is very different from the Bible. For the Muslim the Qur'an is the pure and perfect revelation of God, making Islam the only perfect religion. But in spite of belief in the perfection of the Qur'an's revelation, Islam today suffers from a major crisis of authority. Its "perfect" revelation is ambiguous at many points. Today it seems that any Muslim with an agenda feels free to cite the Qur'an in its support. Osama bin Laden may be the most dangerous example, but he is far from the only one.

Violence and the Qur'an

As mentioned in the previous chapter, one of the most crucial areas of dispute in the Muslim world today concerns the role of violence and warfare in the Qur'an. Some who focus on its warfare texts find fuel for exclusivism, hatred, and killing in the name of Allah. This should not be a total surprise. Westerners reading the Qur'an tend to be appalled at its gruesomeness in places. Because they are grounded in the violent world of the Qur'an, all that some Muslims need to justify suicide bombings and highjackings is the perception of a threat to Islam's position and prestige. As we have seen, Atta and Bin Laden perceived such threats coming from a variety of directions.

Many Muslim scholars, however, especially those living in the West, recognize another side to the Qur'an. They cite recitations that indicate Allah created diverse peoples and cultures for a purpose. Other religious perspectives, therefore, are not to be battled against, but tolerated. And while the Qur'an portrays Allah as a God of vengeance (similar concepts appear in parts of the Old Testament), it has even more to say about mercy, goodness, and forgiveness. Moderate Islamic scholars argue that the violence of the Qur'an is always in the context of self-defense. "Turn them out from where they have turned you out" (2:190-191). Those expelled from their homes may retake what belongs to them (22:39-40). According to Muslim scholar Hafiz Siddiqui of Milipitas, California, Muhammad taught that Muslims were only to attack those in military uniforms and were not to destroy buildings. Such teachings run contrary to the actions of Mohamed Atta.

So the Islamic world is understandably divided in its interpretation. The heart of Mohamed Atta, however, had no such uncertainty. He had a firm and fanatical belief that what he was doing was pleasing to God. But while Mohamed Atta assumed that he was doing God's will, it is helpful to remember that his fanaticism is not characteristic of the vast majority of believers in the Muslim world. In fact, the events of September 11 are so incompatible with the way the average Muslim thinks that millions in the Middle East believe the attacks on September 11 actually represent some sort of Israeli plot. They feel that no true Muslim could have done such a thing.

But the ambiguity of the Qur'an remains a problem. Islam arose in a brutally violent time, and its sacred book bears witness to that ferocity. Muhammad and his followers constantly faced shifting tribal loyalties, betrayals, and misunderstandings. In the process he led his forces into numerous battles, and at times slaughtered what we, at least, would call "innocents." So the use of warfare and the destruction of innocents has some support in the practice of Muhammad himself, the original transcriber and interpreter of the Qur'an. In his defense, however, many would point out that the tribes he eradicated themselves sought to exterminate his faith, making such massacres "defensive actions."

Here we must honestly confront a major difference between the behavior of Muhammad and the teaching and behavior of Jesus, the respective founders of these two great monotheistic religions. Muhammad and his successors clearly used violence in order to expand Islam. Nothing in the teaching or practice of Jesus, on the other hand, gives any encouragement to violence or warfare in behalf of the faith.

Jesus clearly taught that His followers were to turn the other cheek (Matthew 5:38, 39), love their enemies, and riddle those who hated them with kindness and prayer, rather than bullets from AK-47s (verse 44). For Jesus, the highest place in Paradise was not for suicide bombers or battlefield heroes. In His order the last would be first (Matthew 19:30) and the meek would inherit the earth (Matthew 5:5—the teachings of Jesus on this point have echoes elsewhere in the New Testament: Romans 12:17-21; 1 Peter 2:21-23; 3:9).

And Jesus practiced what He preached. When a mob unjustly came to apprehend Him, His friend Peter drew a sword and slashed out in Jesus' defense. Yet Jesus ordered His disciple to put away his sword, even in self-defense (John 18:10, 11). Brought before an dishonest court, He said, "My kingdom is not of this world. If it were, my servants would fight to prevent my arrest" (verses 36, 37).

He placed His life in God's hands, not in those of well-meaning but armed men (Luke 22:42; 23:46).

It is certainly true that the Bible has its own stories of violence in the name of the Lord. In Exodus 15 God stalwartly defends His people, assaulting the Egyptian army with His judicial fury (Exodus 15:7-10). He drowns the hapless armies of Pharaoh in the Red Sea in response to the plight of His people. But such stories do not have the universal force of the Qur'anic commands. Specific actions under specific circumstances, they do not prescribe how God's people should respond to situations with their own efforts.

Furthermore, such stories are not "considered God's own eternal words, as Muslims believe Qur'anic verses to be. . . . Israeli commandos do not cite the Hebrew prophet Joshua as they go into battle, but Muslim insurgents can readily invoke the example of their Prophet, Muhammad, who was a military commander himself. And while the Crusaders may have fought with the cross on their shields, they did not—could not—cite words from Jesus to justify their slaughters" (Bob Woodward, "The Bible and the Qur'an," *Newsweek,* Feb. 11, 2002, p. 53).

Violence and Christian History

The example of Jesus is all the more reason to be horrified that Christians in the past have committed the same kinds of atrocities against Muslim, Jewish, and even Christian dissenters that Muslim fundamentalists are doing today. Infamous in this regard were the Crusades. Its leaders called the perpetrators of its atrocities not "terrorists," but "crusaders" (from the Spanish *cruzada,* "to mark with the cross"), because they wore on their clothing the emblem of the cross.

The Crusades were the product of desperation, at a

time when Islam was transcendent and Christianity was in retreat, not unlike the reversed situation today. While the stated goal of the Crusades was to recapture the "holy places" in Palestine (with the blessing and encouragement of the medieval church), many "crusaders" were little more than common criminals who did not shy away from slaughtering innocent people. (On the way to the Holy Land many of them killed Jews and fellow Christians of the Byzantine Empire, the latter for political reasons.) In the end, exterminating Muslims became as central to the mission as securing control over the holy places. Such history makes it easy for Muslims to blame Christianity for the ongoing abuses of the West.

The Crusades against the "Muslim infidels" were only a prelude to the later crusades against such Christian reformatory movements as the Albigenses, Waldensees, and Huguenots. As grievous as the attacks on September 11 were, they lasted only a few minutes and affected a relatively small number of people. The Crusades of the medieval church against reform-minded Christians lasted for centuries and resulted in the extermination of hundreds of thousands, probably millions. Particularly egregious was the Saint Bartholomew's Day massacre (that began before dawn on August 24, 1572) of the Huguenots, French Christians who preferred the authority of the Bible over the dictates of church leaders. In Paris and the surrounding areas alone, perhaps 10,000 (estimates range from 2,000 to 70,000) found themselves dragged from their homes in the middle of the night and butchered without compunction.

Even America has not always prized liberty of conscience. Christians justified the enslavement of Africans on the grounds that the Europeans were God's favored people. The Salem witch trials show how quickly religious fundamentalism can get out of control, even among people who came to America to gain religious liberty for themselves. As early as 1636 Roger Williams left Massachusetts and founded Rhode Island as a place where Protestant Christians who differed with the state church of Massachusetts could find tolerance and refuge. The founders of Maryland designated the colony as a refuge for Roman Catholics who were unwelcome in the Protestant areas. Later Maryland's leaders encouraged freedom even for Protestant minorities persecuted in other colonies.

A painful recent example of violence among Christians is the horrible genocide that took place in Rwanda. What the media did not so widely portray was the fact that Rwanda is not only one of the most Christian nations in the world, its most common form of Christianity is several versions of evangelical Protestantism. Supposedly "born-again" Christians, including some from my own faith community, aided in the slaughter of those with differently shaped noses or whose skin had a slightly different shade. The genocides of Rwanda demonstrate that when they ignore or distort the teachings and example of Jesus, even the best of "Christians" are capable of mass murder.

Toward a More Tolerant Religious World

In light of both past and present history, it would be easy to put the blame for terrorism on religion in general. A protest sign that appeared on September 12 declared: "No Religion, No War." The sign expressed the conviction that if you could get rid of religious authority and sacred texts, the world would be a better and safer place. In a world torn by division and hatred, any religion that adds to the divisions or fuels the hatreds is part of the problem rather than a solution. Religious types who wanted to change the world have perpetrated some of the most heinous crimes in history.

But would the elimination of religion make the world a safer place? a more tolerant place? History offers a resounding no to both questions. Society has on several occasions attempted to root out all sacred texts and religious authority. One occurred at the time of the French Revolution. In reaction against the excesses of both medieval Catholicism and the French monarchy, the revolutionaries sought to destroy all emblems of religious authority and institutions, from the Bible to the prelates to even the seven-day week! Historians and others often refer to the period as the Reign of Terror! Similar attempts to do away with religious authority occurred under Communism in the Soviet Union, China, and Albania. Few today would want to trade places with the people who endured those regimes.

What we encounter in the French Revolution and Russian Communism was an "elite of the enlightened." They saw the intolerance and exclusivism of the "Christian" West and sought to solve the problem by eliminating the Christian faith. But reaction against religion tends to create a new exclusion that breeds more violence in the future ("We have to stop those narrow-minded people"). To paraphrase the words of Aleksandr Solzhenitsyn: "The line between good and evil does not run between 'us' and 'them' but through the heart of every human being." Terrorism is born in the heart.

I believe that in the wake of September 11 we need, not less faith, but better faith. We don't need less spiritual guidance; we need better spiritual guidance. Instead of "no sacred texts" we could start with a lot more humility in how we handle them. The very nature of the Qur'an, for example, lends itself to atomistic and selective usage. As a series of relatively unconnected references, it is easy to collect all the recitations that say what you want and then use them as authority for the position you already hold. After September

11, students of the Qur'an owe it to the world to be careful and broad-based in their readings. Great damage can result from one-sided readings of a sacred text.

The bottom line is the need for humility. The very greatness of the God envisioned in both the Bible and the Qur'an warns us against the human tendency to think we have attained a complete understanding of Him. All who have sought after God have probably learned something that would be useful to the rest of us. At the same time, no one has the whole package. In the words of perhaps the most educated Bible writer, Paul: "*Our knowledge is imperfect. . . . We see in a mirror dimly. . . . Now I know in part. . . . So faith, hope, love abide, these three; but the greatest of these is love* (1 Corinthians 13:9-13, RSV)." Love, tolerance, and concern for others should be the natural response to a recognition that we all know only in part. None of us have any reason for arrogance. Tolerance, openness, humility, and authenticity toward others must arise from our recognition of our own incomplete understanding of God.

Violence and slaughter, on the other hand, are the refuge of minds who refuse to acknowledge their own ignorance. People such as Mohamed Atta somehow come to believe that God is limited to what they can understand. Paul had no such illusions. "Not that I have already obtained all this, or have already been made perfect, but I press on to take hold of that for which Christ Jesus took hold of me. Brothers, *I do not consider myself yet to have taken hold of it. . . . All of us who are mature should take such a view of things*" (Philippians 3:12-15).

A Challenge to Muslims Today

In light of the above, I would like to offer a challenge to Muslim thinkers, but before I do I want to make it clear that I am not blaming Islam for all the world's troubles. While Islam has failed to solve the problems of the Middle

East, Christianity has fared just as poorly at influencing the West in the direction of peace, humility, and compassion. I offer the following comments in the desire to be helpful. And in the chapters that follow I will offer an even more pointed challenge to traditional Christianity.

I believe that the thoughts and actions of al-Qaeda's leaders ultimately pose a greater threat to Islam than to the West. They seem to have concluded that the result of true faith is material power and wealth that resemble the perceived power and wealth of Allah. In other words, the fruit of true Islam would be world dominance and material wealth. But Islam has not produced this kind of result in today's world. Bin Laden and others have blamed the weakness, the oppression, and the poverty in Islamic countries on the West. But it seems more likely that the problems of the Islamic world reflect a failure to adjust to the rapid changes of the past couple centuries.

To claim material wealth and power as the outcome of true faith is to draw an immediate contrast with the West, which exhibits the very military might and economic abundance that ought to be associated with Allah's cause. No wonder both the Middle East and the West frustrated Atta and Bin Laden! The "infidel" has reaped the very things that should be signs of Allah's favor. So the extremist Islam of Atta and Bin Laden focuses not on producing better people but on seeking to destroy the tokens of the West's ascendancy. Such an Islam can win only by annihilating others. Such an Islam can only increase the world's violence and misery.

But there is another option. The second approach is to acknowledge that Islam becomes the best channel to God when it focuses on faith, not on wealth and power. While Muslims may suffer defeat and poverty in this world, they are the ultimate winners because they have the maturity to ignore the allures of power and wealth. Although Islam may appear to be a loser in the eyes of the West, it is actually a winner, because it is winning human hearts to God by humility, mercy, and compassion.

An Islam that has the strength to renounce power and wealth would also abandon war as a way of achieving spiritual goals. It would free itself to become a spiritual community that would be attractive to all the nations of the world. Such a course might even shame the so-called Christian West into taking the humility and compassion of Jesus more seriously!

If this vision for Islam is the best course of action, Bin Laden's focus on the West and its wealth and power could prove a lethal sidetrack for the faith. Instead of focusing on the spiritual task, people become consumed with destroying the West's power and wealth. Muslim thinkers would do well to reject the al-Qaeda doctrine by renouncing wealth and power as emblems of righteousness. In this way of thinking Muslims should leave the West alone and not covet its riches, but get on with the business of spirituality. If power and wealth is a deception, then the Western way of life will eventually collapse on its own.

I believe that Islam, therefore, can make a major contribution to the world in the wake of September 11 by seizing the path of humility, openness, and spiritual growth. People are hungry for just such a faith. Whether the Qur'an has the capacity to undergird this kind of constructive change remains to be seen. Perhaps the following sura could point the way: "Summon thou [people] to the way of thy Lord with wisdom and with kindly warning: dispute with them in the kindest manner: thy Lord best knoweth those who stray from his way, and he best knoweth those who have yielded to his guidance. If ye make reprisals, then make them to the same extent that ye were injured: but if ye can endure patiently, best will it be for the patiently enduring. Endure then with patience. But thy patient endurance must be sought in none but God " (16:125-127).

Conclusion

The best response to September 11 is a faith that categorically rejects violence in the name of religion. Religious violence improves nothing, but only makes the world a more miserable and a more dangerous place. Extreme forms of religious fundamentalism do more than kill—they divide those who remain and impoverish them, both materially and spiritually.

When Mohamed Atta's plane struck the north tower of the World Trade Center, Bill Feehan was at his Brooklyn office. A 42-year veteran, he had held every imaginable job in the New York City Fire Department, from "proby" to acting commissioner. At 71 years of age he could have retired years before September 11. In fact, one of Feehan's aides had sensed that he was about to call it quits. A memorial plaque for firefighters who died in the line of duty hung in the lobby of FDNY headquarters. It had room for 780 names. During 136 years of existence the Fire Department had bid final farewell to 778 of its number. One day Feehan told a friend, "I want to be out of here before that plaque is full." Little did he know at that moment that on a sunny day in September the list would grow by nearly 50 percent.

On September 11 an aide called Feehan. "Hey, boss! I think you better see this! A plane went into the World Trade Center."

Feehan emerged from his office, looked out a west-facing window, and saw the smoke swirling from the upper levels of the north tower. "Oh, my God!" he said. "Let's go!" He and his team raced across the Brooklyn Bridge to take charge of the fire companies responding to the tragedy. Although they did not know each other, Feehan was about to join Mohamed Atta in the rubble of the north tower. They both arrived there by choice. Bill Feehan and Mohamed Atta met their deaths in the same place because one man chose to destroy and the other to save.

SOURCES

Bacchiocchi, Samuele. "Reflection on Terrorism." End *Time Issues Newsletter,* no. 75, e-mailed on Oct. 16, 2001, from sbacchiocchi@qtm.net.

"The Day That Changed America." *Newsweek,* Dec. 31, 2001/Jan. 7, 2002, pp. 40-71.

Donner, Fred M. "The Sources of Islamic Conceptions of War," in *Just War and Jihad: Historical and Theoretical Perspectives on War and Peace in Western and Islamic Traditions,* ed. John Kelsay and James Turner Johnson. New York: Greenwood Press, 1991.

Glassé, Cyril, ed. *The Concise Encyclopedia of Islam.* San Francisco: Harper and Row, 1989.

Koran, The. Translated from the Arabic by J. M. Rodwell, introduction by G. Margoliouth, Everyman's Library. London: J. M. Dent and Sons, 1909.

McLaren, Brian D. *The Church on the Other Side.* Grand Rapids: Zondervan Pub. House, 1998, 2000.

Premium Global Intelligence briefings posted at stratfor.com.

Siddiqui, Hafez. Phone interview with author, July 31, 2002.

Swartley, Willard. *Slavery, Sabbath, War and Women: Case Issues in Biblical Interpretation.* Scottdale, Pa.: Herald Press, 1983.

Woodberry, J. Dudley. "The War on Terrorism: Reflections of a Guest in the Lands Involved."

Woodward, Kenneth L. "The Bible and the Qur'an: Searching the Holy Books for Roots of Conflict and Seeds of Reconciliation." *Newsweek,* Feb. 11, 2002, pp. 51-57.

————. "How Should We Think About Islam?" *Newsweek,* Dec. 31, 2001/Jan. 7, 2002, pp. 102, 105.

Yahoo! Internet Life, November 2001, p. 77.

4
THE TERRORIST WITHIN

I landed at Schiphol Airport in Amsterdam early on the morning of September 11. It was a beautiful sunny day, and I quickly hooked up with the driver who was to take me to a conference a couple hours' drive away. The countryside was flat as a desktop, but interesting in a Dutch sort of way. After a meal, a nap, and a little reading I headed for the dining room of the conference center around 5:30 p.m. (11:30 a.m. New York time).

I always get a little nervous the first time I am in a large group of new people, particularly when most of them aren't speaking my language. In this case the conference had about 900 attendees from all over Europe, ranging from the Arctic Circle and Iceland in the north and west to Greece and Romania in the south and east. In that setting I was somewhat relieved that the dining room was not crowded. That meant I could eat by myself without seeming anti-social.

I was halfway through my meal when a man from Croatia approached me. I remembered having seen him somewhere before and tried to be friendly in a dazed, jet-lagged sort of way. But quickly I was about to feel a lot more dazed.

"Have you heard the news from America?" he asked.

"What news?" I grunted, thinking I might be in for more explanation than I cared to receive at that moment.

"I just heard that four passenger jets have crashed today in the United States," he said excitedly.

"No way!" I said. "Such a thing has *never* happened before!"

"Two of them crashed into the World Trade Center in New York and the towers collapsed, and another one crashed into the Pentagon!"

"World Trade Center collapsed? The Pentagon?" Now beyond confused, I was suspicious. One of the things I often have to deal with in worldwide travel is all the wild and crazy rumors about stuff going on in America. People want to impress you with their knowledge of things, and often they jump on reports that have no substance in the hope of impressing you. It was beginning to sound like one of those times. "That's impossible. You aren't making this up, are you?" In retrospect, I don't think I was very nice to him.

"It *must* be true. I saw it on CNN. Go see for yourself. They have CNN on a big screen in the room just upstairs."

Still not knowing what to believe, I began to doubt my own reality. Perhaps I was still in a jet-lagged dream and would soon wake up in a bed somewhere in the Netherlands. But the food tasted real enough. Shaking my head, I tried to get the cobwebs out. Hurriedly finishing my meal, I dragged myself upstairs to the meeting room.

Several hundred people had crowded into the medium-sized room to watch a live feed from CNN projected onto a screen. Behind the CNN announcer was a view of the southern end of Manhattan Island in New York City. A huge cloud obscured everything.

Although there were no seats available in the room, someone I knew motioned for the "New Yorker" to take his seat near the front in order to get a good view. Sitting down, I fixed my eyes on the screen for the next hour and a half. The nightmare continued. I peered intently at the screen, looking for signs that the World Trade Center towers were still there, unable to believe that they would have collapsed so easily. Then the network began repeatedly airing a new tape, showing the second airplane impacting the south tower, the fiery explosion that burst out the other side, and the horrified cries of onlookers near the video camera. CNN combined the shot with repeated views of panicked people running for their lives as a great billowing cloud of dust avalanched behind them.

For me this scene cut deeper than for the hundreds of others watching with me. New York was my hometown. I had grown up there and had walked those very streets many times. No matter what the camera angle, I knew its likely location and what it was looking at. I knew whether the camera was pointed north, south, east, or west. Then I considered what I knew about the World Trade Center. On a typical business day about 50,000 people went to work in the twin towers. At any given time perhaps 10,000 tourists would also be there, going up to the viewing decks of the south tower or the restaurant on the 107th floor of the north tower. As the repeated showings of the video made the reality of the collapse clear, the magnitude of the tragedy began to sink in. This was my home town! These were my neighbors and friends. I just *knew* that somebody close to me must have been in those towers, must *be* in their rubble.

Then it struck me! Rolf, a good friend from school days, had asked me how he and his family should spend a week in New York. "Whatever you do," I had told him, "make sure that you visit the observation deck of the World Trade Center and catch the view of New York." September 11 was right in the middle of the week he was supposed to be visiting New York. Although distraught with concern, I could do absolutely nothing about it. I had no way of contacting him from the Netherlands.

Then I took a little comfort when I remembered that I had advised him, "On the day that you visit the downtown, get to the Statue of Liberty ferry first thing in the morning. That is the only way you might get the chance to climb all the way to the top of the statue. Then, when you get back to Manhattan, walk to the New York Stock Exchange and arrange for a tour later in the day. That way you'll get to the observation deck of the World Trade Center in early afternoon, when the view is the best." I realized that if he had followed my advice, he would be looking at the tragedy from Liberty Island, not crushed under the rubble! But I had no way of knowing where he was.

My thoughts went back to the summer of 1999, when I had followed the same itinerary with my family. We got to the World Trade Center in the early afternoon. My wife decided to shop for a coat in Century 21, a discount designer store right next to the WTC, while the kids and I went up to the top. Later I would find out that one of the towers had collapsed right on top of the store and destroyed it. We could all have been there.

All that week in Holland I spent every available moment watching the updates on CNN. The next afternoon I went for a long walk to clear my head. Crossing a bridge over a set of locks on the nearby canal, I watched as they lowered a houseboat to the next level. I then set off through fields of grazing cattle, dodging speedy Dutch bikers on a lovely asphalt path about four feet wide. The landscape was perfectly flat, broken only by occasional trees, the canal, and a couple ponds. It was hard to reconcile that prosperous and peaceful atmosphere with the turmoil still churning inside me. I found I had trouble meeting the eyes of those walking or biking the other way. Somehow I really didn't want to meet anyone, least of all talk to them.

After a couple miles I entered a small, peaceful town and walked along the main street as cars and an occasional truck passed by. There was the typical Dutch country church, a small grassy square with tall trees, and neat, well-kept houses with little gardens along the sidewalk.

Everything looked so tranquil and serene, a strong contrast to the news of a wider world. But it seemed like a great place to find some peace on a shattered day.

At the other end of town I walked past a small school with a grassy playground along the sidewalk. In the playground were about 60 small blond schoolchildren, aged perhaps 5-9, with three or four adult chaperons. A chain-link fence about three feet high and a short hedge stretched between me and the children. Once again a peaceful scene, this time of happy children playing.

Suddenly a horrible thought struck me. What if I were a terrorist? What if I had brought a gun with me, hidden in my clothing? There was no security station on the way into town. Who could have stopped me? I shuddered that such thoughts would even enter my mind. It also dawned on me that no matter how many police, well-trained security teams, checkpoints, or hardened defenses you put together, you can't prevent all acts of evil from occurring. What protected these children from me was not special security teams but my own inner conviction to do the right thing.

Is there a potential terrorist inside of me? I wondered. *Does some sort of straight-line continuum exist between good citizens and mass murderers? Or are the kind of people who fly planes into buildings totally warped and different from me? Are the seeds of terrorism and evil inside all of us?* I thought back to my own beginnings.

I Started Out as a Child

I was born on the Upper East Side of Manhattan . . . when it was poor. It was a home birth on the sixth floor of a walk-up tenement on East 72nd Street. (I have no memories of that event.) My father collected the rent from the other tenants and took care of the boiler, so we lived there free. That helped my parents save money for a home of their own.

When I was about 2 years old they bought a house in New Jersey about seven miles west of Manhattan, but we continued to think of ourselves as New Yorkers. My father did interior decorating for Bloomingdale's (a famous department store in midtown Manhattan), and we continued attending our church in Manhattan. I even commuted to the city for school during my high school years. So New York City was at the center of my life growing up even though we were actually living in New Jersey.

Things were different in those days. People didn't worry so much about letting children explore on their own in the big city. I remember one occasion when I had permission to walk a girlfriend across Central Park (my parents had meetings of some kind) to the Museum of Natural History, one of my favorite hangouts. After the museum closed at 5:00 Susan and I got on the subway and went 10 miles to her house, where my parents picked me up. I was 9 at the time; she was 6!

Perhaps my parents should have been more cautious, but nothing bad ever happened to me on these wanderings. As I got older I would explore the far reaches of the city with my subway pass after school. I'd take friends to skyscrapers, go as close as possible to the top in an elevator, and then find the service stairs to walk up on the roof. Few things are more exciting than being on the roof of a 50-story building with no fence or railing between you and the pavement below. I'm sure they don't allow access like that anymore. But those were the days!

Growing up in New York, I certainly did get into a bit of mischief from time to time. But my life experience had one constant. My family taught me a faith in God that was clear, that spelled out the rules, and that provided guidance for my life. I guess most people would say I grew up in a "fundamentalist" home. I always knew when it was time to be home, for example. And I made every effort to be on time. If

I was even slightly late, my mom gave me a long song and dance about almost calling the police and being *sooooo* worried. Quickly I learned that my life would be a lot easier if I followed the rules.

I came to think of God in similar terms. If you take your bath when you're supposed to, if you go to church at the right time, if you are reasonably nice to your parents, God will be pleased with you. Stay away from alcohol, drugs, and tobacco, and God will approve. The rules were comforting, and they were clear. Don't run in church; you'll scuff the floor. Don't make too much noise. The problem was, though, that there were so many rules I had trouble remembering them all at the same time, so I was constantly messing up in one area or another. Although I tried real hard, I became increasingly sure that God was not pleased with me because of my frequent failures.

One good thing about growing up with religious certainty was that you always knew who the bad guys were. They were easy to spot—the people who didn't go to church. They smoked and drank and swore and believed weird stuff about God (at least different from what I did). They went to nightclubs and shows and places like Las Vegas. The bad people didn't live on my street, but I knew they were out there. Although I didn't run into them every day, when I did I could feel good that I wasn't like them.

There was one exception to the rule, however. I remember "Harry the drunk" who lived a couple of houses away. His apartment was dirty, and he stank. Often he couldn't stand up straight, and he was never able to hold a decent job. So I definitely didn't want to be like him, but he was nice to me. He always seemed happy to see me, and from time to time he would sneak me bags of candy (candy was against the rules unless Mom needed some— then we got some too). Harry was a bit of a problem for me. Although he was one of the bad guys, I liked him and enjoyed being around him.

I guess in some ways I wasn't all that different from the kind of people that get recruited by al-Qaeda. While I certainly wasn't the type to blow myself up or hurt anyone else, I did have a really strong sense that my view of God was right and that a whole lot of people out there had it all wrong. And we're finding out today that the kind of rigid, rule-based religion I experienced can get steered in some very ugly directions. I'm thankful that I never went there, but I realize now that I could have. Terrorism is born in the heart.

Related to this was the fact that I felt extremely out of place in the big picture of New York City. The world, as I came to view it, was so different from the way most people looked at it that I couldn't really talk about my beliefs with most people. They just wouldn't have had a clue what I was talking about. Here I was, interacting on a day-to-day basis with the most cutting-edge place on earth, and yet I would not allow myself to participate fully in the life of the city. Although I had lived my whole life there, I still felt like a stranger in a strange land.

The thing that kept me from going off onto dangerous ground, however, was the example of a couple people in the church in which I was brought up. While many of the members seemed severe and unfriendly to children, there were a couple of major exceptions. A sweet old German woman named Mrs. Daxenbichler (I learned how to pronounce it a long time before I learned how to spell it) spent quite a few Saturday afternoons teaching me how to understand the Bible. She seemed different than most of the church people I knew. Mrs. Daxenbichler seemed really happy and really enjoyed being a Christian. I took hope from knowing her, but I often wondered what she was so happy about.

The other positive role model was a man named

Zestermann (obviously I spent a lot of time around Germans). He always had a smile for me and told me that I would be a big success someday. Quite a joker, he played a pretty mean honky-tonk piano at church socials (under the somewhat disapproving gaze of some of the more "spiritual" types). I'll never forget the day that the church let me give the sermon. I don't know what they were thinking (I was 11 years old at the time), but I worked really hard on it. It bombed anyway. I labored for 56 minutes (the number embarrasses me to this day) to say something useful, and when it was over, I was looking for a hole in the ground to disappear into. I felt that I had really blown it big-time.

As I was standing at the church door afterward Mr. Zestermann came up to me. "Could you step outside with me for a couple of minutes? I'd like to talk to you," he said.

We walked up the street toward the corner of Park Avenue and 87th Street about 20 yards away from the church. He always called me "Jonnie" when he was in a good mood.

"Jonnie," he said, "I just wanted to tell you how much I appreciated what you said today. It was just so important for my life. I want to thank you, and I hope you'll get a chance to speak again soon."

It's unbelievable, the power of encouragement. Mrs. Daxenbichler and Mr. Zestermann exhibited a different kind of religion, one based on understanding, encouragement, kindness . . . and fun. It was new for me. I liked it. But something inside of me felt it was somehow wrong. While I didn't mind being happy and having fun, I just wasn't sure if it was OK! And I just couldn't enjoy myself if I thought God wasn't pleased.

When I was in college, a speaker came for a week and emphasized one thing only. He suggested that God was more interested in making friends than in condemning people. Furthermore, he encouraged me to put my effort into knowing God rather than doing stuff to avoid His disapproval. The man's message intrigued me. Although very different from the way I had been raised, it was compelling. I decided to check what the Bible really had to say about the subject.

Here is where I made the first major change in my spiritual life. When I was a kid, I had a tendency to ignore Bible texts that didn't seem to support what I was thinking. I was operating from a selective approach. Now I decided to try three new strategies in my study of the Bible. 1. I would take a "big picture" approach to Scripture. I would be open to the whole Bible, as it reads, rather than picking and choosing whatever fit with beliefs I already held. 2. I would ground my understanding on what is clear in the text, rather than trying to make the less clear things say what I wanted them to. 3. I would pay special attention to the ideas of people who disagreed with me. Maybe some of the "bad guys" knew something I didn't.

The last point reminded me of what I call the "Saddam Hussein syndrome." Saddam Hussein's advisers tend not to disagree with him, since most of the ones who do wind up dead! As a result, he doesn't get a lot of good advice. People tell him what they think he wants to hear. So when I listen to what Muslims, Jews, atheists, Buddhists, Catholics, evolutionists, Baptists, or others have to say about the Bible, there's a chance I might learn something!

Soon I learned to test my ideas about God by the plain teachings of the Bible in its widest context. When I began to do this, I became amazed at what I had missed. My narrow perspective about God began to change, because the God of the Bible didn't fit with the deity others had told me about. Let me share with you what I learned from that study.

The Big-Picture God of the Bible

The first, and larger, half of the Christian Bible is called the Old Testament. The Old Testament starts with the creation of the world and treks through the history of Israel back in ancient times (the part of history we call B.C.). Unlike the Qur'an, which reflects a 20-year period in a small corner of Arabia, the Bible is the collective memory of God's interaction with many groups of people during thousands of years.

As I explored the big picture of the Old Testament I discovered that everything centers on four major acts of God: the creation of the world, the story of a worldwide flood, the Exodus from Egypt, and the return of the Jews from Babylonian exile. As I read the accounts of these actions, I learned a number of interesting things about God, things that I hadn't known when I was growing up.

Creation, the Flood, and the Exodus

The first three events bunch up right at the beginning of the Bible. My study revealed that the three stories exhibited a common pattern. For example, the biblical writer repeats the language of the Creation account (Genesis 1 and 2) again in the Flood story (Genesis 6-8).

The same thing happens with the account of Israel's "exodus" from Egypt under Moses, an incident well known from Hollywood movies such as *The Ten Commandments* and *The Prince of Egypt*. This story (found in Exodus 12-15) describes Israel's escape from Egypt in the language of the Creation and the Flood (Exodus 14:21, 22: the italicized words in the sidebar parallel the language of earlier events).

As I compared these three biblical events (the box on the next page is my attempt to simplify what I learned), I found a surprising and purposeful similarity in the way Scripture describes them. The pattern of God's actions seemed to say a lot about who He is and how that might affect my life. Let me briefly share with you the five most important things I learned from the comparison below.

CREATION	THE FLOOD	THE EXODUS
Chaos	Chaos	Spiritual chaos
Waters cover earth	Waters cover earth	Red Sea
Wind (Spirit) over waters	Wind blows over waters	Wind blows over waters
	Ark passes through waters	
Waters divided		Waters divided
Dry land appears	Dry land appears	Dry land appears
Image of God		Firstborn
Dominion over earth	Animals afraid of Noah	Dominion over Canaan
Fruitful and multiply	Fruitful and multiply	As the sands of the sea
Adam	Second Adam (Noah)	Creation of a people
Formed from the earth	Man of the soil	Land of Canaan
Put to sleep		
Woman formed	New earth formed	
Shamed by fruit of tree	Shamed by fruit of vine	
Paradise		Canaan
Tree of life		Manna
Test		Test in wilderness
Serpent		Serpent
Covenant implied	Covenant renewed	Covenant

Learning From the Pattern

1. God Is Consistent. The stories about Creation, the Flood, and the Exodus portray God behaving according to a consistent pattern. You could say that God's past actions depict what He will do in the future. Thus what God did at the Creation, for example, sets the pattern for what He did at the Red Sea. The two events are very different, and yet the same God is at work in both instances. So I learned that God is not arbitrary, as in some pagan concepts of God, and I could count on Him to relate to me in a consistent manner.

2. God Is Not Predictable. While God is consistent, He is not predictable. Although He approaches people, events, and circumstances in similar ways, His later activities do not carry out every detail of the pattern. We find no serpent or tree of life in the Noah story, for example. The Exodus is not a worldwide event, no one is put to sleep, and no one gets shamed by what they eat or drink. So not all the elements of the Creation story repeat themselves in the stories that follow. God is consistent, but not mindlessly so.

Here is where the big-picture view of the Bible began to move me away from my youthful overconfidence and has relevance to the problem of religious terrorism today. I found out that God's consistency is not a mindless, point-by-point thing. Religious extremists think they know exactly what God is thinking and what He will do in all circumstances. But the Bible teaches us not to put God in a box. We must let Him be Himself. The Bible teaches that He is consistent enough to be known, but too unpredictable to be controlled. To assume, as the Taliban and some branches of the Christian Right do, that nothing ever changes with God is to assume the opposite of what Scripture demonstrates.

3. God Is Creative. God's later actions further develop His earlier ones and often enhance them. While acting consistently on the whole, God is not afraid to do things differently from time to time. His revelation of Himself increases as His people become able to grasp it. God is not limited to the details of His previous patterns. The Bible portrays a creative God who operates freely within the limits of His overall consistency. He might even be friends with someone I don't particularly like!

4. God Meets People Where They Are. God always works within the time, place, and circumstances of those who receive the revelation. He designs His messages to make sense within human history and experience. Thus God "speaks the local language." He is not an ivory-tower God like the deity of Plato or Muhammad but is deeply engaged in the lives and experience of those who follow Him. As a result He meets people where they are. This view of God is a major difference between the Bible and the Qur'an, as we will see.

5. God Has Moral and Spiritual Goals. In the Exodus story the language of God's action shifts from literal to spiritual (from the physical devastation of a worldwide flood to the mental and emotional devastation of slavery, for example). Thus the chaos of the waters around the earth is parallel not only to the Red Sea but also to the slavery of the Israelites. The Israelite situation was a spiritual mess (Exodus 1:8-22). They needed God's creative power to get them out of Egypt (Exodus 3:7-10).

The basic scenario and language of the earlier stories remain, but Scripture uses them in a figurative, spiritualized form. While the Bible is full of history, wars, and cataclysmic events, they exhibit a moral purpose rather than a political one (see next chapter). To assume that "God is on our side" in matters of war and politics usually represents a misreading of the Bible's purpose.

The New Testament and the Messiah

The climax of the Bible's big picture appears in the last part, the New Testament. God is just as flexible and creative in the New Testament as we saw in the Old. The Old Testament prophets pointed forward to a fifth major act of God (because of space reasons, we didn't cover the fourth, the return of the Jews from Babylonian exile). In that act He would send a Messiah to right the wrongs of our world. The Old Testament describes that Messiah as a prophet like Moses (Deuteronomy 18:15, 18), a king like David (Jeremiah 23:5, 6), and a conquering hero (Zechariah 9:9, 10).

From such texts we could easily get the impression that

Jesus would be a powerful king who would dominate the political forces in His world (many Christians act as if that were the case). But Jesus used these texts for a moral purpose rather than a political or economic one. His kingdom was not like human nations (John 18:36, 37). Warfare was not the way to attain spiritual goals (verses 10, 11). Jesus' kingdom had to do with character development, spiritual growth, and enhanced relationships with others and with God (Matthew 5:21-48; Luke 17:20, 21). While Jesus' kind of kingdom would change the world, it had nothing to do with the weapons of this world (2 Corinthians 10:3-5).

I have gained great respect for the Qur'an and the dedication of those who practice its faith with mercy and compassion. And I have no doubt in my mind that the Qur'an represents a great advance on the religious sensibilities of the tribal religions it replaced. And while some Christians may disagree, I believe the God portrayed in the Bible "has not left Himself without witness" (Acts 14:17, RSV) among those who follow other paths. God recognizes the sincere worship of people in every nation as directed to Himself (Malachi 1:11).

Nevertheless, the Qur'an still leaves God distant from us. The deity of the Qur'an does not speak our language (unless we have learned Arabic). Nor is He deeply involved in our existence. Instead, He is distant and easily seems uncaring and even vengeful. By way of contrast, the God of the Bible is a practical deity who meets us where we are (principle 4 above). Unlike the distant God of Muhammad, He is deeply engaged in the human condition.

But the Bible goes one step further. It claims that Jesus of Nazareth, a human being born in a stable of Bethlehem, raised in Egypt and Palestine, was none other than the living incarnation of God's person (Hebrews 1:1-3). One who was God from the beginning took on human flesh (John 1:1-3, 14).

Such a God is deeply concerned about our situation. He taught and healed and comforted people in the lowliest of circumstances. As a "humble" God, He never ordered His followers to use weapons in His behalf. Instead He commanded them to love their enemies (Matthew 5:44), just as He did when He died for the very ones who crucified Him (Romans 5:8-10).

A Challenge to Christians

While in the previous chapter I offered a serious challenge to Muslim thinkers, now I confront traditional Christianity in an even more pointed way. After all, Muslims who take up arms in behalf of their faith can at least point to their own sacred texts for justification. But what justification does the Bible offer for the way the West flaunts its power and wealth in the world? Where in the teaching and practice of Jesus do we find any basis for advancing the Christian agenda through military, political, or economic means? We could understand a Muslim missing God's call to mercy and compassion in the violence of the Qur'an, but what excuse can the follower of Jesus offer for overlooking God's call to openness, grace, love, and peace?

Yes, I know that the United States and Europe are no longer truly "Christian" nations. The West today is not pursuing a religious agenda, but a political and economic one. But in the light of Christianity's past, in the shadow of the Crusades and the Inquisition, can we really expect the Muslim world to understand the distinction between Western action and Christian faith? When they look at Rwanda, Iraq, Afghanistan, and Israel against the background of Christianity's record, where is the spirit of Jesus?

I believe that traditional Christianity has failed in its own struggle to grasp and demonstrate the teachings and attitude of Jesus, who humbled Himself and stepped down from heavenly wealth, power, and glory (Philippians 2:5-8).

Although He could have exploited His divine status for His own advantage, as earthly rulers do, He chose instead to become human and take on the role of one who serves for the benefit of others. He demonstrated in human form that God is not greedy, violent, or self-absorbed. God is not like us—and that is a good thing. Jesus demonstrated in human form, therefore, that we find the answer to violence and terror not in power and wealth, but in humility, authenticity, and forgiveness. Traditional Christianity has failed as badly as Islam to provide the solutions to the world's problems. At the same time it has strayed even further from its roots than Islam has. In the next chapter I explore the fundamental reason for Christianity's inability to see its own failures and offer a solution that is grounded in both the Bible and the traditions of Islam.

Conclusion

When it comes to knowing the God of the Bible, a little tentativeness is always advisable. It was the lack of such tentativeness that killed four ATF agents and led David Koresh and his followers to destruction. A similar failure drove Mohamed Atta to do the ghastly "work of God" that was September 11 and Osama bin Laden to plan and encourage it. All three men thought they knew exactly what God wanted them to do and exactly how to bring about the result that He had in mind. And all three believed that God's ways and their own thoughts were in perfect harmony.

Frankly, I find this amazing. We don't expect anyone to paint the "final painting," one so perfect that no more art needs to be produced. Nor do we expect "the final and complete discovery" from any scientist. Yet we have the capacity to think we have fully understood God, as if He were far more limited a concept than science or art!

Many use religion and God-talk as a tool in behalf of their

own agendas. But, as the psalmist says (sidebar), they have made a basic error: they thought that God was just like them, just as rigid, unbending, and at times hateful as they were.

But the Bible actually portrays a God who cannot be put into a comfortable human box, a deity who is not predictable. Whenever we think, speak, or write about God it is critical to maintain a reverent tentativeness about our conclusions. We must leave God the freedom to be Himself. While openness, honesty, authenticity, and humility are very much part of today's philosophical landscape, a call for these virtues is more than just political correctness. The very words of Scripture mandate it. Some in the past have misused the Bible for political or economic gain, but upon more careful examination it portrays a God who is very much unlike ourselves.

In the wake of September 11 it is imperative that we combat terrorism with the weapons of this world; but it is even more critical that we fight it with the weapons of truth. Hatred, disparagement of other religions, boastful self-confidence in one's absolute correctness—these are the ultimate roots of terrorism. A faith that exhibits the compassion, mercy, justice, and love of God with an appropriate humility and openness will be a major part of our recovery from the event that changed the world.

SOURCES

McLaren, Brian D. *The Church on the Other Side.* Grand Rapids: Zondervan Publishing House, 1998, 2000.

Paulien, Jon. *Centered in God.* Hagerstown, Md.: Review and Herald Pub. Assn., 2003.

Wright, N. T. The *Climax of the Covenant: Christ and the Law in Pauline Theology.* Minneapolis: Augsburg Fortress, 1993.

5
My Own Personal Jihad

For a few harrowing weeks during the autumn of 2001 a group of U.S. officials believed that something even more horrible than September 11 was about to happen. They believed that terrorists had obtained a 10-kiloton nuclear weapon (about half the destructive power of the bomb that destroyed Hiroshima in 1945) in Russia and were planning to smuggle it into New York City. Detonated in lower Manhattan, such a device would kill about 100,000 people and expose 700,000 others to sickening doses of radiation. It would flatten everything in a half-mile diameter, a much greater ground zero than that left by September 11. Counter-terrorism agents went on their highest state of alert. In October several governmental agencies received a report about the threat, including the Nuclear Emergency Search Team, based in Nevada.

The source of the report was an agent code-named DRAGONFIRE. His claim that the 10-kiloton bomb came from the Russian nuclear arsenal was supported by a report from a Russian general, who believed that his forces were missing a 10-kiloton weapon. Adding even further to the official concern was the longstanding suspicion that several portable nuclear devices might have vanished from the Russian stockpile. So even though intelligence experts considered DRAGONFIRE himself as of uncertain reliability, his report made sense and triggered alarm in high places. But the official reaction remained highly classified, and officials were at great pains to make sure the secret did not get out.

According to one U.S. official, "it was brutal." While it would be the natural human instinct to warn those who were in greatest danger, the White House decided to keep the matter secret so as not to panic the people of New York. Senior FBI officials never received any warning about it. Former mayor Rudy Giuliani says he knew nothing about the threat. Certainly the people of New York slept peacefully, not knowing that a nuclear sword might be suspended over their heads.

In the end, counterterrorism experts found nothing to confirm the report and concluded that DRAGONFIRE's information was false. Russian officials now claim that they have accounted for their nuclear stockpile and that terrorist nukes, if they exist, would have to have originated else-where. But the diminishing of this particular threat has not allowed people in the intelligence community to sleep any better. They have been forced to confront their worst fear: if terrorists did manage to smuggle a nuclear weapon into New York City, or any other city, there wouldn't be a whole lot anyone could do about it. In the late spring of 2002 the movie *The Sum of All Fears* brought a similar concern to public consciousness.

America's War on Terrorism

In the wake of September 11 all kinds of frightening scenarios suddenly sound more plausible. While the United States and its coalition allies have struck back hard at the ter-rorist infrastructure all over the world, the terrorists have not simply gone away. Thousands of al-Qaeda terrorists survived the battles in Afghanistan and have melted into the hills or across the border into Pakistan. Sympathetic tribes in west-ern Pakistan have sheltered many and helped others get out of the country. Al-Qaeda has instructed its operatives to shave their beards, adopt Western clothing, and do whatever it takes to stay undetected until such a time as they can set their missions in motion again.

So while relative calm set in after September 11, few think that America has seen the last major terrorist strike. Sooner or later al-Qaeda and its sympathizers will make another attempt to shake America's confidence and terrorize its population. The American government is so certain of another attack that it has assigned 100 civilian government officials to 24-hour rotations in underground bunkers in order to provide a "shadow government." This shadow government would be prepared to take over if the next major terrorist target should turn out to be Washington, D.C. One counterterrorism official warned ominously: "It's going to be worse, and a lot of people are going to die. I don't think there's a———thing we're going to be able to do about it."

While al-Qaeda has been in retreat since September 11, the very nature of its strategy means that it is far from finished. The vast number of targets available and the hidden nature of the attackers makes defense a highly perilous endeavor. "If you're throwing enough darts at a board, eventually you're going to get something through," a Pentagon strategist commented. "That's the way al-Qaeda looks at it."

For the executive and legislative branches of the U.S. government, the battle against terrorism has become something of a holy war. President George W. Bush's speech to Congress on September 20, 2001, had all the overtones of a spiritual conflict. At stake was more than the lives of innocents. September 11 had been an attack on the American way of life and the liberties that make America the envy of oppressed and suffering peoples all over the world. So the assault on terrorism has taken on the spiritual quality of jihad. It is perceived as a battle in defense of all that is true and right and just.

The nation is expending vast amounts of money, intelligence assets, and personnel to track terrorists at home and abroad. In a sense the United States is attempting to surround itself with a protective net. But as *Time* pointed out on March 11, 2002, "all nets have holes." America long ago designed its security system to fight Soviets rather than suicide bombers and hijackers. On September 11 the CIA had dozens of Russian-language specialists, but only one Afghan analyst. As a result, September 11 caught the American intelligence community completely by surprise. "It was an abject intelligence failure," said one White House aide.

It seems that with the fall of the Soviet Union CIA officials lost interest in the dirty task of human espionage, relying more on electronic eavesdropping and satellite imagery. But the decision had a price. Let's face it, really good spies, the kind that can penetrate terrorist cells, are not usually the nicest and most reliable people around. A "kinder, gentler" intelligence operation would use "cleaner" practices than hiring local thugs and informants. But the result of this shift in policy was that America's most highly trained spies turned out to be less skillful at infiltrating al-Qaeda than a 19-year-old boy from California named John Walker Lindh.

So the cutting edge of America's own jihad begins with the battle to upgrade its intelligence about the enemy's plans, purposes, and location. Without that, the only safe defense is one that anticipates every possible angle of attack, particularly against assets for which we do not yet have adequate defenses in place, such as water supplies. To make matters worse, every mile of the U.S. coastline is a potential entry point for nuclear, chemical, or biological weapons. In a sense, eradicating terrorism is like finding a way to detect and apprehend criminals *before* they commit their crimes.

September 11, while a terrible day for the United States, did not really threaten the nation's existence. But were al-Qaeda able to acquire weapons of mass destruction, the threat would become real and ongoing. In a taped broadcast after September 11 Osama bin Laden warned that he intended to destroy the United States. Nuclear, chemical, and biological weapons offer the means to attempt such a goal. So America's struggle is no longer about bringing justice on the heads of those who planned September 11, but about preventing something even worse from taking place.

In order to stop future September 11s, the United States has determined to destroy as much of the al-Qaeda network as possible as quickly as possible. Even if it proves impossible to destroy the terrorist network completely, the goal must be to damage it thoroughly. The objective is to destroy at least some of the weapons of mass destruction and intimidate the terrorists in ways that will keep the rest immobilized for fear of detection.

Since any weapons of mass destruction could take multiple paths into the United States, the U.S. must be able to reach deeply into many or most of the 60 sovereign countries in which al-Qaeda has been known to operate. Overt and covert operations strike with stealth and suddenness to disrupt the military, economic, and communication capabilities of the terrorist network. Nothing short of all-out jihad will do. The very existence of the United States of America is at stake. The potential consequences of failure are so great that the nation cannot afford a limited or halfhearted response. But this war is much more behind the scenes than out in the open. A brief look at one covert level of this holy war may be of interest.

The Role of the Internet

The terrorists' greatest asset against America's counterattack may be the very system that has transformed American life during the past decade: the Internet. The same Internet that has enhanced human efficiency and enjoyment has also proved to be an ideal tool for planning, communicating, and carrying out terrorist attacks. The weapons of the terrorists on September 11 may have been low-tech, but they could not have planned or carried out the attacks without the Internet.

"No Internet, no Bin Laden" may be an overstatement, but it is not far from the truth. Investigations after September 11 indicate that every aspect of the planning and coordination of these attacks "bore the marks of the information revolution." "They used the Internet, and they used it well," said an FBI official a week after the attacks. How did the FBI know? They had come across hundreds of e-mail messages exchanged by the hijackers before the attacks. The messages had originated from personal computers, computers in libraries, and Internet cafés.

How did the terrorists come to use the Internet and e-mail? For years they had made much use of cell phones for planning and coordination. But it didn't take them long to discover that wireless telephones were like a welcome mat to the National Security Agency (NSA), America's prime eavesdropping agency. Terrorist after terrorist found themselves nailed after revealing their location through cell phone calls. So cell phone technology proved to be more harm than good to the terrorists' cause.

Why use the Internet then? Aren't e-mails and one's use of Web pages open to anyone with the desire and the ability to snoop in other people's stuff? Yes and no. Most Internet correspondence is easily intercepted. Yet the terrorist organizations found several ways to dumbfound the electronic surveillance of those fighting against them.

First of all was a development known as secure encryption. Encrypted messages on the Internet are far safer than cell phone calls. In fact, right now encryption is light-years ahead of the code breakers at the NSA, CIA, and FBI. For all practical purposes today, encrypted messages are impossible to unravel. If that were not so, credit card transactions over the Web would be impossible. And price is not a problem. One can download the latest encryption software for free from anywhere in the world, even the caves of Afghanistan (thanks to satellite modems).

A second aspect of terrorist communication is a bit more low-tech. Al-Qaeda has become expert at steganography. Steganography is the art of hiding the unusual or the secretive in obvious places, attached to normal, everyday transactions. For example, terrorists can embed maps and photographs of terrorist targets, along with instructions of how to carry out operations, in chat messages, Web sites, even pornographic photographs! If these things are being enshrouded in things that normally pass over the Internet, the counterterrorist has no search engine or other labor-saving device to pick out terrorist transmissions from all the others. It is necessary to break down individual, normal-looking messages and hope that you hit something significant by chance. And even if you do, how would you recognize that this particular map, this particular photograph, this particular ambiguous chat message or e-mail contains instructions for carrying out a terrorist attack? Spying just got infinitely harder.

Third, and related to the above, is the sheer mass of electronic messages that moves across the Internet every day. The average office worker exchanges dozens of e-mail messages a day, while key people may go through a hundred or more. Multiply that by the hundreds of millions who are online around the world daily, and you have a volume of messages too vast for spy agencies to sift through effectively. Encrypted, normal-sounding messages lost in the vast background noise of the Internet are almost impossible to pick up. It is truly about finding an electronic needle in an electronic haystack.

Recently another level of cloaking has become common for al-Qaeda. Its remaining leadership has created a Web site containing organizational information and encrypted instructions. They distribute the Web site by CD-ROM to key operatives around the world. Then they post it on local servers with some nondescriptive code, usually numerical (so American intelligence can't find it) and distribute the site address to local members via encrypted e-mails. Since any Web site can be viewed from anywhere around the world, having it on many servers makes tracing the origin of the site nearly impossible. Shutting down one site doesn't prevent its sprouting up in several other places.

All of this helps to explain how the CIA failed to raise an alert when two of the September 11 hijackers paid for their airline tickets with credit cards in their own names. Since the authorities had placed both men on terrorist "watch lists" weeks before, it should have triggered an alert. But the sheer volume of electronic transactions, combined with poor coordination among the various intelligence agencies, led to a failure to see the obvious. The result was the untimely death of nearly 3,000 people and the traumatization of a whole nation, if not much of the world.

Many Americans take comfort in the large amount of effort and expense that the U.S. government is investing in the battle against terrorism. But that comfort may be misplaced. The NSA is America's most important agency for the collection of information about terrorist operations, yet it is losing its ability to target the communication systems increasingly used by terrorist cells and operations. In light of this it is no surprise that we had no advance warning of September 11. It is a lot easier to track people after you know that they've done something bad than before they do it. Because of the Internet, power is moving away from large institutions such as governments, churches, and universities and into the hands of the little people. And not all of them use that power for good (any more than the large institutions did).

Today it is possible for people scattered all over the world to form a tight network of common interest, even though they have never met in person. They can find each other, exchange ideas, lay plans, and carry out common actions. And there is little that any government can do about most of it. For those who want or need to keep secrets, times have never been better. America's jihad is going to be a long and difficult battle.

The Setting for Personal Jihad

I find America's struggle mirrored in one of my own. Some 30 years ago I visited the Riverside Church in the Upper West Side of Manhattan one Sunday with a couple friends. Riverside Church, along the Hudson River, has one of the five largest classical organs in the world. Being an organist myself, I could never get enough of hearing it. The organist that day was Frederick Swann. He was internationally famous, with dozens of recordings.

When the worship service ended, I took my friends up on the platform for a closer look at the organ. And since I knew quite a bit about such things, I began to explain some of the different features of the organ. As I talked about the organ, my audience began to grow. Unfortunately that encouraged me to expand on the story a little. And the audience got even bigger. Then suddenly I realized that the people weren't watching me anymore.

Instead, their attention was on something behind me. When I turned around I found myself standing face to face with Frederick Swann himself. He looked me in the eye and said, "You'd better get your facts straight, sonny, before you open your mouth." Then he walked away.

That day I began to realize that something deep inside of me made it hard for me to be real, to be authentic. Instead of being honest and truthful I had played up to the audience in order to polish up my own image (which turned out to be a stupid way to do it). Now I felt humiliated, ridiculous, and downright ugly! I wasn't angry at Swann. How could I be? He was right about me! Upset with myself, I hated whatever it was inside of me that was trying to hide my own ignorance and stupidity behind a facade of brilliant repartee. Not wanting an incident like that ever to happen again, from that day I decided to make the struggle for authenticity my own personal jihad.

What does the Islamic concept of jihad have to do with my personal life? Historically, jihad is much less about killing people who disagree with you and much more about the personal struggle toward an authentic faith. In fact, the concept of jihad has at least three meanings within Islam. First, it refers to the struggle of all who believe in God to be faithful to Him and to live good lives. Second, it involves the struggle to understand and interpret Islam. And third, it indicates the sacred struggle to defend and advance the cause of Islam. The root meaning of the word, however, is closer to the first meaning than the last.

This may be confirmed, for example, by a tradition (*hadith*) about Muhammad addressing his followers upon their return from a battle (although some Islamic fundamentalists deny the authenticity of the tradition). He tells them that they have now returned from the "lesser jihad" (the physical battle between soldiers) and must take up the "greater jihad," the inner struggle for genuine submission to God. It is arguable that the use of the term *jihad* for waging war is post-Qur'anic, and that the Qur'an uses the term exclusively in its natural sense.

I believe therefore that jihad, rightly understood, moves us away from terrorism and the mass murder of "infidels." Instead, jihad is about the battle with self to become a better person, not only on the outside, but also on the inside. Read in that light jihad involves combating the evil in ourselves before turning our attention to the evil in others. If we can defeat the terrorist within, there is some hope we can overcome the terrorist without.

The Bible addresses this same concept in the striking military terminology: "Though we live in the world, we do not wage war as the world does. The weapons we fight with are not the weapons of the world. On the contrary, they have divine power to demolish strongholds. We demolish arguments and every pretension that sets itself up against the knowledge of God, and *we take captive every thought to make it obedient to Christ*" (2 Corinthians 10:3-5). Here we see a clear contrast between the two interpretations of jihad or holy war. True holy warfare is not about material weapons such as AK-47 rifles, M1A1 tanks, or F-15 fighters. Instead, genuine jihad is a battle with self, a battle toward authentic living, a battle to become more loving and kind in service to God and others. I believe that the greatest of all jihads is the struggle to be real.

The Struggle to Be Real

As illustrated from my own experience earlier, the struggle to be real—to be authentic—is a difficult one. What do I mean by the words "real" and "authentic"? It is when the outside and the inside are the same. Only then will the things we reveal about ourselves reflect the real truth about ourselves. The Bible addresses the difficulty of this goal. "*The heart is deceitful above all things* and beyond cure. Who can understand it?" (Jeremiah 17:9). Our inner selves attempt to mask who we really are, even from ourselves! Why is it so hard to be authentic? We may find some clues in the insights of psychology. It seems that human beings have built-in defense mechanisms that kick in the minute we're under pressure emotionally or psychologically.

Let's suppose I am teaching in a large classroom. At one point in the class Randy Johnson walks in the door with a base-ball in his hand. For those who have never heard of him, Johnson is six feet ten and can throw a baseball 101 miles per hour with his left hand! Now imagine that he takes exception to something I told the class, and launches his 101-mile-per-hour fastball right toward my nose. Would I stop teaching and ponder my response? "Well, let's see, Randy Johnson just launched a 100-mile-an-hour fastball toward my nose. I suppose I should start thinking about getting out of the way!" I don't think so! Much faster than you can say "Randy Johnson" I would have my hands up in front of my face to block the attack on my life! I wouldn't need to think about it—I wouldn't even be conscious I had done it until after I felt the sting of the baseball on my wrists. The reaction would be automatic.

Just as we have physical natural defense mechanisms, so we have emotional and psychological ones. If someone says something hurtful about us, we may react defensively with-out even being aware that we have done so. At a basic level, such psychological mechanisms of defense are self-decep-tions. When things go wrong, when we fail at something important, or when we come under verbal or emotional attack, we move quickly to our own defense and craft an "image," whether we intend to or not. If knowing the truth will make us feel bad about ourselves, most of us would pre-fer not to know the truth.

Psychologists label one type of defense mechanism "displacement." Displacement occurs when you express anger in one situation that is really directed at some other person or situation. For example, the boss yells at you at work. But you don't talk back to the boss, because it will get you fired, so you go home and yell at your spouse instead. Your spouse doesn't want to mess with you right now, so later he or she shouts at the children instead. The children, taught not to talk back to their parents, deal with the situation by kicking the dog in frustration. That's called "displacement." The situation can come full circle only if your boss comes over to dinner and gets bitten by the dog!

Another defense mechanism goes by the name of "sublimation." It happens when a person has socially unacceptable urges. Sublimation helps the individual channel those unacceptable desires into behavior that is socially acceptable. For example, a young man might have a murderous anger toward his father. But it is socially unacceptable to murder your father. So the young man funnels the urge into a more acceptable path—he may go into hunting or become a football player. Society even commends violence in those fields! Or the son might even become a surgeon. Now don't get me wrong. I didn't say that all hunters, football players, or surgeons have a murderous anger toward their father! I'm simply pointing out that many of us do not fully understand the reasons we do what we do.

According to specialists at the Minirth-Meier Clinic:

1. Defense mechanisms are automatic reactions to frustration and conflict. They move into action without our intention. Like our response to flying baseballs, we have all experienced similar reactions at an emotional level.

2. Defense mechanisms are unconscious. Most of

the time we don't even know we're employing them. They are inner ways of protecting us from painful emotions and experiences.

3. Defense mechanisms exist to maintain a false sense of self-esteem and to avoid anxiety. By nature we avoid probing our innermost motives for fear that we will find something that produces guilt and makes us feel even worse about ourselves.

Do We Have To?

If genuine authenticity seems impossible in the normal course of events, we may be tempted to stop seeking it. Wouldn't it make more sense to find a mask that won't slip off when we're in trouble? And wouldn't it be an "ideal world" if everyone could totally, successfully hide themselves? But though it may seem attractive at first glance, closer inspection reveals that inauthenticity is extremely destructive.

Inauthenticity in relationships means avoiding issues and failing to communicate. But that is a recipe for long-term disaster. When it comes to finances, inauthenticity involves not making a budget, not keeping track of expenses, not planning for retirement, and not knowing where the money will come from to repay what we borrow. Few people survive that kind of financial "planning" for long! In the area of health, inauthenticity leads to eating whatever you want, sitting around all day, ignoring all the rules of health, and still hoping to live to 100 without a single illness. But that's not real life. Inauthenticity can kill you, and you'll probably be the last one to know it before you go.

So faking it is not a useful option, whether we're talking about individuals or nations. But being real is not easy to do. First of all, as we have seen, self-deception comes pretty naturally to human beings (Jeremiah 17:9). Through self-deception we craft an image, not only for others, but even for ourselves. There is an even deeper issue, however. The root cause of such "image-building" seems to derive from a deep inner perception that we are hopeless and worthless. We are afraid to learn the truth about ourselves, because then we'll feel even worse! I'd like to share with you my own personal jihad to overcome these two challenges. I'll begin with my struggle against self-deception.

The Struggle to "Know Myself"

Again and again in my life I have been sure that I was being real only to discover a hidden phoniness right in the midst of my most authentic efforts. I can be completely authentic at one point and 24 hours later find myself faking it again. In the process I've learned a few things that have been helpful. Here's the skinny on my personal jihad toward authenticity.

1. Spend serious time with the Bible. A major step in my struggle for authenticity has come through general reading of the Bible, particularly the stories about its major characters. You see, the Bible does not present individuals such as Abraham, Moses, and David as heroes or flawless saints. The spiritual "saints" of the Bible were real people with significant flaws. In fact, most Bible characters seem even more messed up than you or I are.

The story of Esther is an example of what I mean. Because the hard edges of the story are not that obvious in translation, Christians have tended to portray her as the brave follower of God who won a "beauty contest" to become queen of Persia. But according to the Hebrew text Esther did more than walk down a runway to be chosen queen. She somehow proved that she was better in bed than all the other girls (Esther 2:13, 14). It is also clear that she did not practice her faith while living in the palace (Esther 2:10; 5:12, 13; 7:3, 4). How do we know? Her own husband didn't know that she was Jewish. Authentic Jews are very hard to hide, especially in the bedroom and the kitchen! But regardless of her spiritual defects, she ended up being in the right place at the right time to accomplish God's purpose.

An honest reading of the Bible, therefore, has given me the courage to seek the truth about myself, no matter how scary such a search might seem. If God could accept Esther and David (if you're not familiar with the sordid details of his life, read 2 Samuel 11-21), there's certainly hope for you and me.

2. Experiment with a spiritual diary. The concept of a spiritual diary or journal has also helped me in my struggle toward authenticity. In my experience God has used the self-reflective activity of keeping a diary to draw things up from the depths of my inner self in ways that nothing else can. I call it my "book of experience." What I like to do is get a blank journal page in front of me and ask God such questions as: "How do You feel about the way I treated my son yesterday? my wife? What can I do to reconcile these two colleagues who are estranged?" Then I begin to write and let it take me wherever it will.

Often I will find myself in places I hadn't planned to go, but to which God was clearly leading me. For example, I may come to the realization that I talk too much in small groups, fail to express caring to my students, or expect too much from my children. In the process I discover flaws and weaknesses in myself that I knew nothing about. Or I detect trends in my life that I would miss if I did not take the time to reflect on them in this way.

3. Practice authentic prayer. A furthering dimension of my battle toward authenticity has emerged through what I call "authentic prayer." By that I don't mean just any kind of prayer—only the type of prayer that is willing to risk all. Authentic prayer says, "I want the truth, no matter what the cost." Experience has taught me that when you say such a thing to God you will definitely get a clearer picture of ultimate reality, but it will also usually demand something. Throughout history a commitment to truth has cost many individuals family, job, reputation, and even life. So authentic prayer has opened me to significant risk.

But in my struggle for authenticity, I find it helpful to be even more specific, something like this: "I want the truth *about myself* no matter what the cost." You see, "truth" can be very abstract and theoretical. But that can become a substitute for a more practical kind of truth. Knowing the truth about myself is very different from truth in the abstract. And God is good at helping me here. The Lord is like a "heart" surgeon that gets down deep inside (Hebrews 4:12, 13).

4. Accountability. The deepest level of authenticity may be the most critical to success in knowing oneself. Sometimes the only way I can find reality is through the eyes of another human being. Often that happens in a small group or a classroom. As I hear others telling the truth about themselves, I connect with what they are saying and realize that I have some of those same faults myself. But for me the best level of accountability is to open myself up to a carefully selected friend who loves me and cares deeply about me. No friend is so faithful as the one who cares enough to tell the truth.

You see, I am somewhat of a public person. Many people are a bit afraid of me because I have a strong personality. The average individual tends to tell me what they think

I want to hear. But I don't want to end up like Saddam Hussein. I've worked very hard to cultivate friends that I can trust, and encourage them to be honest with me. It is one of the best ways to bypass personal defense mechanisms.

But what if you don't have any close friends? What if you have no one that you would trust with the deepest anguish of your heart? Then find a good professional counselor to help you. Counselors train to help people open up and discover the deeper truth about themselves. Taught to be good listeners, counselors can often detect when you are playing games of self-deception. Life is too short to waste in inauthenticity.

The Issue of Self-worth

We all face a serious dilemma. If we are to understand our own self-deception, we must first of all have a genuine feeling of self-worth, a sense of personal value. When our self-worth is low, the most natural thing in the world is for us to hide behind an image rather than submit to reality. So what can we do to elevate our perception of self-worth? People try a number of remedies, but none of them work for long.

Three Ways to Approach Life

Many seek life in the "bottom-line" approach. We value ourselves in terms of home, cars, and bank balances. The more we have, the more we're worth. Or as the bumper sticker says, "When things get tough, the tough go shopping." The bottom-line approach *does* feel good, but the sense of value doesn't last. Our precious toys scratch, rot, rust, and crash. And in the end, "You can't take it with you."

Others focus on self-development or performance. We seek value by succeeding in sports, games, work, or hobbies. Or we knock ourselves out to get higher degrees, more prestigious positions, or greater fame and fortune.

Yet even if we achieve our fondest dreams, we discover that the sense of worth doesn't last. Star quarterbacks get old and frail, beauty queens get old and wrinkled, and teachers get old and mindless. Achievement is real, but the feeling of value doesn't last.

Third, people also define life in terms of "who you know." We find value in terms of what other people think of us. When others praise us, promote us, love us, and generally think well of us, it makes us feel worthwhile. Teens blossom when another teen thinks of them as uniquely valuable and special. But as good as a meaningful relationship feels, even this approach has its limits. People may discover things they don't like about us, change their minds, move away, or die. Rejection hurts the most where one has loved the most.

What then? Is there no way out? Is there no secure path to a genuine and lasting sense of worth? Possessions, performance, and people are good things. They are part of the spice of life, but they are not life itself. If one could find true life in possessions, performance, and people, professional basketball players would be the happiest individuals on earth. After all, they make millions of dollars a year, are admired by people all over the world, and have all the romantic options anyone could possibly want. Why then is drug abuse a major issue in professional basketball? Why are some players so angry and dysfunctional? Because life—real life—cannot be found in money, performance, and people alone.

Jesus *Is* the Answer

But all is not lost. If we could find a friend who knows all about us, yet loves us just the way we are (so we know that they will not change their opinion of us), who is genuinely valuable (a superstar), and who lives forever (so we won't be bereaved by death), we could have a strong sense of self-worth and meaning in our lives. And that feeling of self-worth wouldn't be hostage to the ups and downs of the stock market, the highs and lows of our daily performance, or the moods and whims of our friends and relatives.

That's what Jesus is all about. The Bible tells us about a person who is worth the whole universe (He made it), yet knows all about us and still loves us even as we are. And when He died on the cross, He established the value of a human person. Because the Creator of the universe (more valuable than everything in the universe, including all the toys and superstars we often worship) decides to die for you and me, it places an infinite worth on our lives. And since the resurrected Jesus will never die again, my value is secure in Him as long as I live (I'll take forever!).

Have you ever seen a billboard or a bumper sticker with the words "Jesus Is the Answer"? Perhaps it made you wonder what the question was. For me the question was: How can I have a true sense of worth that will empower my personal struggle toward authenticity? I have found that sense of worth in Jesus Christ. If I am that valuable to the greatest person in the universe, then it doesn't matter whether I'm rich or poor, great or small, famous or ordinary, and it makes no difference what anyone else thinks of me. To have Jesus is to have life, even in poverty, sickness, and bereavement. Jesus *is* the answer after all.

And above all, in the context of a relationship with Jesus, I can pursue a rigorous jihad against my own inauthenticity. I can be truly humble and honest about my shortcomings, because my essential value is not at stake. Thus I don't need to strike back every time someone gets in my way or unloads their anger against me. True serenity can come, not through disengagement from the world, but by seeing all that happens in the context of my relationship with Jesus.

Conclusion

What does all this have to do with my challenge to traditional Christianity in the previous chapter? Simply this: People have used the name of Jesus to slaughter Muslims (the Crusades), Christians they didn't agree with (the Inquisition), and to enslave and marginalize Christians of a different skin color (slavery, apartheid). Somehow taking the name of Jesus did not prevent Christians from slaughtering other tribes in Rwanda and other denominations in Yugoslavia, or from offering support to Hitler.

Traditional Christianity has too often been a massive exercise in corporate denial. Those taking the name of Jesus have too often been blind to the darkness within. If Jesus is to be the answer in today's world, a lot of people are going to have to find a way to look beyond Christianity and most Christians if they are to have any hope of finding Him. What a tragedy if some of the very institutions that uplift the name of Jesus should turn out to be the essence of what the Bible calls antichrist!

From September 11 on the world has cried out for healing. And there is hope for that healing in Jesus. But business as usual is no longer appropriate in the hallways of faith. I invite people of all faiths to proclaim jihad, not against people we disagree with, not against other faiths, but against ourselves, against our own willingness to tolerate pride, arrogance, and self-deception. Any other spiritual quest will fall short of the healing our world so desperately needs. It is only by conquering the terrorist within that we can have any hope of putting an end to the terrorism without. True authenticity is worth a holy war!

SOURCES

Calabresi, Massimo, and Romesh Ratnesar. "Can We Stop the Next Attack?" *Time,* Mar. 11, 2002.

Esposito, John L. "Jihad: The Struggle for Islam," in *The Religion Factor: An Introduction to How Religion Matters.* Ed. William Scott Green and Jacob Neusner. Louisville: Westminster John Knox Press, 1996.

Johnson, James Turner. *The Holy War Idea in Western and Islamic Traditions.* University Park, Pa.: Pennsylvania State University Press, 1997.

Paulien, Jon. *Knowing God in the Real World.* Boise, Idaho: Pacific Press Pub. Assn., 2000.

Peters, Rudolph. *Islam and Colonialism: The Doctrine of Jihad in Modern History.* The Hague: Mouton Publishers, 1979.

Premium Global Intelligence briefings posted at stratfor.com.

Scheer, Robert, and Aseem Batra. "The Terrorists and the Net." *Yahoo! Internet Life,* November 2001, pp. 86, 87.

BASIC STEPS TO AUTHENTICITY

1. First, accept by God's grace that you are significant and valuable in Jesus Christ. Only those who know their worth to God would ever dare to examine the darkness within. The event of the cross defined human significance. Out of that sense of value comes the drive to be real.

2. Know your true condition. No one can be authentic unless they are willing to face the truth about themselves.

3. Accept the truth about yourself. As you go through the process of self-discovery, embrace the results of that process as a true statement of your condition.

4. Take the truth about yourself to God for forgiveness and release. Tell God what you have found out about yourself no matter how painful that might be. There's something about bringing the truth about yourself into the open that takes away its power. And since God already knows the truth about you and is committed to receiving you in the light of the cross, you have no reason to fear.

5. Seek continually to grow in authenticity. Authenticity is a process, not a state. No human being could become totally authentic in a moment. Our nerves could not handle it. So God feeds us the bad news a little bit at a time. And in the courage of our newfound sense of self-worth, we can face a little bit more each time.

6
LIFE IS SHORT—PRAY HARD

September 11 was a day when it seemed as if everyone in the world was either in New York or trying to reach someone there. On that day, checking your e-mail became a matter of life and death for many. By 8:45 a.m. Ron Bruno was sitting in his apartment, already dreading the day ahead: a meeting he was not prepared for, coworkers already e-mailing the day's fresh woes, a lunch date he would need to cancel—*again.* In other words, the morning was par for the course in Manhattan, stressful and complex. Then he heard the news. A Boeing 767 had crashed into the World Trade Center, an event too horrible to make sense. Like a robot, he tried to go on with his business for a while, unable to grasp what was occurring and what was still about to happen.

To the rest of the world, Manhattan Island might seem a rather small piece of real estate. But the World Trade Center, which loomed so large on TV screens around the world, was not even visible from the street in most parts of Manhattan. Bruno, who lived and worked in midtown, seven miles away, was himself more likely to see the World Trade Center from a jet arriving or departing New York than he was to view it from the ground. The tragic event at the southern tip of the island exploded into the world's consciousness through the mass media. And most New Yorkers became aware of it in the same way.

By 8:55 a.m. the first of many questions of concern about Bruno arrived in his e-mail in box. It came from his cousin Bev in the New Jersey suburbs. "How far are you from there? Are you at work? Please tell me you are safe."

Bruno started an irritated response about the great

divide between midtown and downtown, then erased it and tried again. "I'm fine. Both the apartment and my office are far from the WTC, so no worries. How are you?"

Then another jet took aim at the second tower. It was becoming apparent that the crashes were not accidents. As he turned on his TV in time to see first one tower and then the other fall, his in box began to ding repeatedly with new mail. E-mail would turn out to be the best way for friends and family all over the world to verify the one piece of news that was most important to them: Ron Bruno was alive. As it happened, a whole lot of people wanted to know.

Bruno's regular band of far-flung correspondents, such as his cousin Remo in southern Italy, made up the first wave of messages. "In this moment I'm watching on TV. Our prayers go to you and the family. I have no words to continue." His friend Alberto, in Florence, Italy, didn't hesitate to show emotion. "Ron, I am a lot preoccupied for you! Are you near to the danger? Please send me your notices!"

E-mail preserved their distinctive voices and lent variety to what was becoming the only question Bruno could definitely answer. Cousin Joe, a financial journalist in London, laced his concern with a little black humor: "You just want to make sure the people you care about are OK. I mean, who knows, you might have been off on some dumb early shopping trip to Century 21 [a popular discount department store near the towers]." Bob, a college buddy living in Chile, wrote: "I haven't felt this pit-of-the-stomach the-world-is-mad feeling since I caught you watching the *Challenger* explode over and over again. NOBODY is safe, but do you HAVE to live at ground zero? Is all that excitement . . . worth your paying for the country's political screwups with YOUR life?"

Bruno decided to get back to him later with a more nuanced response. On September 11 all he could write was a simple "yes" and "hmmm." By the next day Bruno began hearing from people at an even greater relational distance, and for once he was not irritated. Unfolding events shattered the mutually agreed-upon information blackout between him and an ex-romantic interest: "Hey, man . . . you OK? I felt like I wanted to say hello when I heard about this."

His early responses reflected the limited level of his ability to understand and absorb the day's events. "Yep, I'm fine. I live about seven miles from there, and all is safe uptown." The sheer volume of e-mail concern led him to cut and paste those two sentences repeatedly. A lawyer friend of his found a half-burned scrap of letterhead from a WTC-based firm on his lawn across the East River in Brooklyn. While the wind would not carry the stench of the inferno to midtown for another day, e-mail was Bruno's shield against events, protecting his family and friends from worry, and himself from total terror.

Bruno's friend Denise, who also lived in midtown, wrote: "You'd better make sure you have cash; the ATM lines are a nightmare here." He decided that he'd better venture offline and out. On the bank line, what began as a simple exchange of news among strangers became a hot political debate, fueled by an elderly woman spewing hate against "all Arabs." Yet as Bruno walked home he saw a merry band of preschoolers skipping down the sidewalk with a couple nannies trailing behind. Two stonemasons were busy restoring a broken-down stoop. It was a day of clear blue skies, laughing kids, and thousands of dead people Bruno couldn't see. As reality didn't mesh with what he was seeing on TV, he became more confused and angry and felt a growing sense of isolation.

At home he had another wave of e-mails, this time from less frequent correspondents: a girl he used to tease in eighth-grade algebra, high school friends he hadn't seen since the last reunion, professional colleagues. Many of them lived far away and weren't sure if he was even in Manhattan after all those years. Oddly enough, Bruno found catharsis with these e-mail acquaintances, more than with those closer to his life, whether in town or on the phone.

"I had a fight on the bank line that made me sick," he told a woman he hadn't laid eyes on since the Reagan era. He described to a college roommate the "inspiring civility" of the Upper West Side supermarket crowd he encountered on the way home, "even as they busted open boxes of Perrier in the aisle and hoarded pasta and cornflakes." Both the civility and the hoarding were due to the fact that thousands of people had lost their lives seven miles down Broadway. Seven miles was starting to sound very, very close to Bruno.

E-mail proved to be much more therapeutic than the phone. The typical phone conversation on September 11 was punctuated by long periods of silence and repeated musings along the line of "I can't believe this is happening." It was too soon to talk things through. E-mails, on the other hand, gave Bruno opportunity to reflect on the complexity of his sadness and uncertainty. His keystrokes were often hurried, but the words kept pouring out, and they helped. He suspected that after September 11, many of these correspondents would drop out of his e-mail in box for months or even years, but at the crucial moment they were with him, and that was all that mattered.

As the day continued Bruno shuttled between the TV in the living room and the computer screen in the bedroom. Television doled out the images while e-mail helped to process them as part of a new reality. An acquaintance from out of town summed it up later: "It seems I left one life—my own, the city's, the world's—and came back in another." Television announced the day that changed the world, a new world had come at last. Bruno gathered his e-mail and "slouched toward it."

As our experience with e-mail teaches us, writing is a marvelous way to develop relationships even though we may not be physically together. And social scientists have noticed an interesting feature of e-mail. People somehow feel safer with it than they do with any other type of communication. They are willing to say things that they would never put in a formal letter or say to someone's face. So e-mail has become a major factor in relationships during the past decade or so.

In the case of Ron Bruno, e-mail was a soothing way to process that which could not be understood or even imagined. When phone calls offered little solace, e-mails, even with people he hardly knew, provided an outlet for his feelings and a strong sense of connection to the wider universe, one he probably would not have gotten from those in his immediate circle around New York.

Online With God?

For me, e-mail provides a strong analogy to the way prayer has functioned through the centuries. Prayer helps one to find a center in the midst of the normal chaos of contemporary life, and even more so in times of great tragedy, such as September 11. There comes a strong sense that we are not alone, that no matter what takes place, there is an ultimate purpose to it all, that out there is One who cares deeply about us and whose presence can be felt from time to time.

A Titanic Analogy

But how do you have a serious relationship with someone you cannot see, hear, or touch? How do you have a relationship with someone who is not physically there? I have wrestled with this concept for many years, and the events of September 11 didn't make it any easier.

A few years ago I observed something that has helped me make some sense of such questions. The movie *Titanic* earned a lot more money from theater admissions than any other movie up to then. What was the reason for such "titanic" excitement? One of the main factors was that millions of teenage girls in North America became smitten with the handsome young male lead, Leonardo DiCaprio. Many went back to see the movie several times. Some claimed to have seen it more than 40 times! What were they doing? They were developing a relationship with someone they couldn't see, hear, or touch!

Wait a minute! you may be thinking. *Weren't they seeing and hearing him in the movie?* Yes, in a sense they were. But watching a movie is not quite the same as meeting Leonardo in person. The movie was only a *witness* to the reality that is Leonardo. But how do you know Leonardo DiCaprio even exists if you've never met him, heard him, or touched him? Well, for starters, the movies he has made testify to his existence. You hear about him on radio or TV, you read about him in magazines and newspapers. No one doubts his existence, even though few have met him.

The existence of God is secure on a similar basis. Whereas millions will testify to the existence of Leonardo DiCaprio and the influence he may have had in their lives, *billions* through the centuries have testified to the existence of God, including the testimonies found in sacred texts. The craze over Leonardo DiCaprio illustrates how you can have a real relationship with someone you cannot see, hear, or touch. You can have a relationship with Leonardo if you spend time with the various witnesses about his person. Thus you can read about him, talk to people who know him, and sample his own testimony about himself on TV, radio, or in a magazine. For many young women, at one point their relationship with Leonardo was the most significant thing that had ever happened to them, even though they had never met him in person.

So it is with God. If you are seeking a real relationship with Him, you can start with the primary witness about Him, the Bible. It contains the record of His impact on people during an extended period. There you will meet Jesus, whom Scripture describes as the clearest expression of God's character in the whole history of the human race (John 14:6-9; Hebrews 1:1-3). We can meet the invisible God in still other ways. You can talk to people who know Him and hear their descriptions about His impact in their lives. And you can experiment with the kinds of actions that have helped others find God.

When you think of all the time and energy that many young women expended to get to know a movie star, it is not surprising that in the aftermath of September 11 more and more people are making the search for God a priority in their lives.

The Building Blocks of Relationship

I remember when I first met my wife. She is quite pretty, so I noticed her right away, but wasn't particularly impressed until a week later, when we had a chance to talk for about a half hour. As we started to go our separate ways I was uncertain exactly what to do, so I offered a handshake (go ahead, laugh at me)! That handshake was like an electric shock. I didn't know how she felt about me, but I decided then and there to pursue this particular relationship (she admitted months later that she had felt the electricity of that handshake too). So I began to look for opportunities to spend time with her.

The next week I saw her starting to walk home (her place was about two miles from where we were). Gallantly I offered her a ride in my supercool new car. She declined, saying she wanted to enjoy the nice day on foot. Deciding that it was too early in the relationship to walk with her for a stretch, I let her go that time. The next week she accepted my offer of a ride. My car was a 1972 Opel Manta, sort of a poor man's BMW, from Germany. It had four on the floor and was a pumpkin-orange color (I've never seen a car color like it since) with a black hood, a black vinyl top, and lots of black stripes. In the back of my mind I said to her, "Prepare to be impressed!"

When she saw the car she piped up, "What's that, a Pinto?" For those of you who don't remember that particular car model, if you drove one you hoped no one noticed. If you didn't, you felt insulted if anyone compared your car to it! I was so deflated. My cool little sports car a Pinto? Oooh, that hurt. But I figured she didn't know much about cars, so I got over it quickly. Then I invited her to join me the next day for an outing to the Cloisters, a twelfth-century monastery that the Rockefellers had brought over from France and rebuilt. The monastery sits on the highest point in Manhattan, at the exact opposite end of the island from the World Trade Center. It is a very beautiful site.

Week after week I spent more and more of my spare time with her. We walked through the parks of New York City. Sometimes we had picnic lunches, other times pizza. We visited all the great tourist sites of New York City, including the Statue of Liberty, the World Trade Center, the New York Stock Exchange, St. Patrick's Cathedral, the Museum of Natural History, and so on. The bottom line was that we spent hours and hours talking, listening, and doing stuff together. In the process we explored our personal histories and shared our hopes and dreams and plans for the future. We discussed our families—the good, the bad, and the ugly.

What I didn't realize at the time is that we followed the classic formula for building a relationship. It involves spending lots of time doing three basic things: (1) talking heart to heart, (2) listening carefully and attentively, and (3) doing meaningful things together. Take away any of the three, and a relationship will not be healthy. Spend no time together at all, and the relationship will die.

Some people write about this in terms of building the "infrastructure" of a relationship. That means taking the time to connect with each other's thoughts, feelings, hopes, and dreams. When thinking of marriage, "building an infrastructure" involves sharing mentally, emotionally, and spiritually before you share physically. And when it comes to God, it means taking time with the building blocks of spirituality. As when I courted my wife, relationship with God does not happen by accident. It is the outgrowth of intentional response to the tokens of His presence in our lives, even though those tokens may seem few and far between.

A Living Relationship With God

A major disincentive to consistent prayer is the sense that it is only one-way communication. We talk to God, but He never answers back. Or does He? How can we know His answers to our prayers? Does God still speak with a living voice today, or do we need to guess His will through the chain of circumstances that follow prayer? Would you know God's voice if you heard it?

The Voice of God

Let me tell you about one time that God seems to have clearly intervened in my life. It began with an invitation to speak to a few hundred people at Lost Lake Wilderness, a remote area in the north central part of the state of Washington. The site was about 35 miles from the nearest small town and about 15 miles from the nearest road on my map of the state.

I like the change of pace that traveling provides and enjoy seeing new places and meeting new people. So normally when a trip approaches, I look forward to it with a certain amount of anticipation. But that wasn't the case this time. Instead I had a general sense of unease, almost dread, and I just couldn't figure out what was causing it. Why was it that every fiber of my being kept saying that I didn't want to go on this trip?

Once we had started out toward Lost Lake through Indiana, Illinois, Wisconsin, Minnesota, and South Dakota, the general unease began to crystalize into a more specific sense of danger on the highway. However, I didn't say anything about my feelings to anyone else in the family. I just became a little more alert while driving. Also I didn't complain (as I often do) that my wife was content to let me do most of the driving!

Things passed fairly uneventfully until we reached the mountains of western Montana. The interstate highway began the climb into the Bitterroot Mountains. The small van we owned at the time was very reliable, but it had a little four-cylinder engine that slowed us to about 25 miles per hour on steep upward grades. At one point a truck came along behind us, moving just slightly faster than we were. He pulled out to pass, and when he got alongside me, the road flattened out a bit and my van surged forward. For a minute or so we seesawed back and forth, sometimes the truck gaining on me, then the van regaining some of the ground.

Suddenly I saw yellow flashes of light to my left and realized that the truck driver had lost track of my presence next to him. He was signaling his intention to move over into my lane. Although I honked my horn, his engine was much too noisy for him to hear me. As he started to edge over into my lane I honked again, but was eventually forced right off the highway. Slowing down on the sloping grass next to the road, I managed to keep control of the van, then eased back onto the highway. Later on, when the road leveled off again, I caught up with him and cranked it up to about 85 miles an hour in order to pass him quickly. I wasn't taking any more chances on his lane changes!

I seriously doubt that he was ever aware that he had run us off the road. The interesting thing is that 200 yards past the point where he unknowingly forced us off the highway there was a guardrail. Had he pulled over at that point, we would have had no place to go. His truck would have crushed us against the guardrail or possibly even knocked us over it and down the embankment. After this incident I finally told my wife about my impression of danger on the highway.

"Well, in that case we had better be *real* careful from now on," she replied.

"No, it's over," I responded. "That was what God was trying to warn me about. I'm sure everything will be OK from now on."

I now experienced a total release of anxiety that was just as real as the previous impression of danger. Somehow I knew that the threat was past and that the rest of the trip would be reasonably uneventful. And it was. I call the kind of thing I experienced an impression. I feel a conviction that certain things are going to happen or that I should do one thing or another.

Now, I'm not suggesting that God always warns or protects us. Ironically, it was on the way home from that very same trip that I was happily driving through South Dakota with my cruise control set at 65 miles per hour (the exact speed limit for that stretch of road). To this day I wonder why God gave me no advance warning about that police officer in South Dakota! Though my speedometer indicated that I was traveling a steady 65 (that part of South Dakota is very flat), his radar gun said I was traveling 77. And he had absolutely no sense of mercy. It turned out to be a most expensive traffic stop for me. Perhaps it was an example of God's sense of humor!

These incidents and others have led me to believe that God is very real. The Lord seems to be just as willing to communicate today as in Bible times—if we are willing to listen. I do want to be clear about one thing, though. I'm not talking about audible voices here, but simply the sense or impression that something is true or that I should take some course of action.

Does that mean that all impressions come from God? Of course not. Impressions can come from a variety of sources. But I do think that some impressions can certainly have their source in God, and that He intends for them to help us navigate through a variety of life situations, particularly those not directly addressed in the Bible. But some impressions are downright evil, whether you think of them as originating from the devil or simply our own darkness within. The Bible sometimes calls such impressions to do the wrong thing temptations.

A third source of impressions come from neither God nor the entity the Bible calls Satan or the devil. Some impressions may simply arise from the murky depths of our own inner selves, something I sometimes call my "inner fog." Still others may reflect the expectations of other people, such as our parents or spouses. So if we want to be attentive to God's inner voice, we need to be able to recognize the difference between the various kinds of impressions. And in a world filled with religious extremism, it is especially important that we be able to evaluate religious impressions. Terrorists and others often determine their actions by such impressions.

I've developed the following procedure for listening to God. You might want to try it out for yourself. When you decide to pray, have a pencil and paper ready with you. Then after you have finished your prayer, wait quietly. Write down whatever thoughts and ideas come to your mind during the next five to 10 minutes. This is somewhat like spiritual brainstorming.

When I do this, I discover that a large percentage of the thoughts and ideas that pass through my mind at that time are irrelevant. In fact, some of them may be downright silly, as is fairly typical with any brainstorming process. But some of them are promising. So I check them out. If I feel impressed to visit someone, I visit them! Or if something insists that I make a phone call, I do it! And should I have an insistent urge to shop in a particular place, I go there and see what happens. In other words, I test the impressions and observe the results.

Whether or not an impression came from God, I think, can be discerned by the results of trying it out. As I look back on past experiences I can often tell when God was leading and when I was going my own way. By reviewing my responses to various impressions and their results, I develop a sharper sense of how God has chosen to lead me personally.

Suppose, for example, I feel impressed that I need to contact certain people or pray with them. When I contact them they keep remarking about the exceptional timing of the visit, or how badly they needed a visit right then. This would suggest to me that God's hand was behind the impressions that led me to do good at just the right time. I have had many days like that. As I realize that God is alive and active, and that He cares enough to guide me in even the minor details of life, I have a growing sense of purpose and fulfillment.

But things don't always work out that way. Sometimes I have an impression that I should contact certain people and the reaction is less positive. The individuals may scratch their heads and have no idea why God might want me to visit them just then. The incident may even get me or them into trouble! When the results of a particular impression do not work out for good, that impression likely came from a source other than God.

For me, then, the key is to try out my impressions, or at least the ones that aren't obviously stupid or contrary to the Bible. I experiment with them and keep track of the results. Through the years I have learned to distinguish the voice of God from some of the other voices in my head. I believe that God assumes a certain way of speaking with people, one that you gradually come to recognize and to trust. His voice comes to me with a particular "accent." To gain this recognition did not come easily. It took time and careful attention. But the joy and fulfillment that this relationship has brought me was well worth the time and effort.

Can you enter into a process like this when you still have doubts whether God is really there? The Bible responds to such questions with the invitation to "taste and see" (Psalm 34:8). How can you possibly rule out the divine element in human existence if you have never attempted to seek God for yourself? According to the Bible, God has chosen to make Himself known to those who seek Him with all their hearts (Jeremiah 29:13).

To those who are willing to accept instruction from God (John 7:17), who approach Him with singleness of purpose, He reveals Himself in meaningful ways. An interesting by-product of the September 11 tragedy for many who had ignored God in the past is an increased desire to seek Him.

Conclusion

The events of September 11 left many with a sour taste about God. Some concluded that it would be better not to believe in Him than imagine a deity who could stand on the sidelines while terrorists flew fuel-laden airliners into buildings full of people. But as life teaches us, the universe is far more complex than the simple answers we often prefer. In the next chapter we will take a look at that intricacy and the implications it may have on the search for God.

SOURCES

Bruno, Ron Bel. "Re: Are You OK?" *Yahoo! Internet Life,* November 2001, pp. 73, 74.

Paulien, Jon. *Knowing God in the Real World.* Boise, Idaho: Pacific Press Pub. Assn., 2000.

DEVELOPING A RELATIONSHIP WITH GOD
based on
Jon Paulien, *Knowing God in the Real World* (Boise, Idaho: Pacific Press Pub. Assn., 2001), pp. 66-81.

Nutshell strategies for talking with, listening to, and working with a God whom we cannot see, hear, or touch.

Talking to God
Some strategies to increase the effectiveness of prayer:
1. **Any way you can.** There is no single right way to pray. People described in the Bible prayed standing up, on their knees, and flat on their faces. They prayed with their eyes open and with them shut. And they prayed with hands folded or outstretched. What counts in prayer is not the right style, but connecting with God.
2. **Writing is good.** Like e-mail, written prayers are a good way to focus the mind.
3. **Go to the core.** Prayer becomes truly meaningful when it is open, heartfelt, genuine, and deeply relevant to our experience.
4. **Allow God to answer.** Don't rush. Take time to listen.

Listening to God
The place to most clearly hear the voice of God today is in His written Word, the channel through which He spoke most directly to the human race. Ways to enhance the study of the Bible:
1. **Make it relevant.** Finding a relationship with God almost always begins with a felt need of some sort. So it is best to begin Bible study with sections that speak to the problems we are wrestling with from day to day.
2. **Focus on Jesus.** Since God interacted most clearly with the human race through Jesus, a focus on the person of Jesus is crucial for human beings who want to know God (the four Gospels—Matthew, Mark, Luke, and John).
3. **Take your time.** The Bible rarely reveals itself to casual readers. Don't rush.
4. **A record of great thoughts.** Write down or enter into your computer the insights that God gives you from time to time as you search the Bible.
5. **A spiritual diary.** Such a diary helps you listen to God directly, have open-ended reflection, and keep track of trends and spiritual growth.

Common Interests
The most effective kind of faith brings God into every moment of the day.
1. **Sharing faith is not an option.** Expression deepens impression. When you discuss things you are learning about God with others , it helps to strengthen and confirm your own growing faith in Him.
2. **Stretch the limits.** Take some risks in your walk with God. Go on a mission project, plant a garden and dedicate the proceeds to charity, etc. Shared risk enhances intimacy.
3. **Walk the talk.** Apply the Bible's counsel for everyday life seriously and put it into daily practice. Experiment with how you treat people or your own body and mind while following the example of Jesus.
4. **Act on impressions.**

7
GOD'S INSCRUTABLE BUT
TENDER MERCIES

For many people on September 11, survival seemed to be an accident of location and timing. George Sleigh was a manager at the American Bureau of Shipping on the ninety-first floor of the north tower of the WTC. He was on the phone in his office when he heard the roar of jet engines. Looking out of his window, he had just enough time to think, *The wheels are up, the underbelly is white, and man, that guy is low!* It was 8:46 a.m., and a Boeing 767 airplane was headed toward him at 500 miles per hour with 92 people and more than 50 tons of fuel aboard. The jet exploded into the building at floors 93 through 98 just above him. The walls, the ceiling, and the bookshelves in his office crumbled.

Crawling out from under the rubble, Sleigh looked up at the exposed beams and concrete underside of the ninety-second floor. What he didn't know at the time was that his concrete ceiling was the floor of a giant tomb for more than 1,300 people. Not a single person survived on any of the floors above him, but on his floor and below nearly everyone lived to see another day. The line between life and death was as thin as a steel beam or a concrete slab.

Counting heads, Sleigh discovered that 11 of the 22 employees at his office were on duty at the time. None were injured. Other than his area the office was largely intact. Sleigh went back to get his briefcase. The closest stairway was blocked, but the second was open. Heading down for several floors, he and his colleagues found the going quite peaceful. There was nobody behind them. By the time they reached the middle of the tower, Sleigh's office was engulfed with flames. Fifty minutes later, having become separated from his colleagues in the increasingly crowded conditions on the staircases (more and more people were evacuating and they had to leave room for the fire fighters who were charging up to fight the blaze), Sleigh left the building and was loaded—bruised, bloody, and covered with dust—into an ambulance. "Get out, get out," a police officer yelled. "The building is coming down."

It was 9:59 a.m. The south tower was collapsing. A survivor from the highest point on the north tower, Sleigh was on his way to Beth Israel Hospital.

"Sometimes I think it was God's providence that spared me," he said. "Other times I wonder why me and not others. I realize I am a very fortunate man."

He was not the only fortunate person. Amanda's story was a lot less dramatic, but more tragic. A regular at the Windows on the World, she was a dark-haired, dark-eyed beauty who had found life and its relationships to be confusing at best and frightening at worst. Windows on the World was a classy restaurant on the 107th floor of the north tower of the World Trade Center. Floor-to-ceiling glass provided spectacular views of the city. From more than 1,300 feet up in the air the cars, buses, and taxis resembled tiny insects crawling their way around a miniature city.

Amanda had three favorite views from the restaurant. The best view was to the east, where the East River bridges loomed in magnificent miniature over the water. The next-best was to the north, where the Empire State and Chrysler buildings were pointed counterparts to the hundreds of giant faceless boxes that make up the midtown Manhattan skyline. And the third view was to the southwest, where the toylike Statue of Liberty sat right in the middle of the bay that marked the outlet of the Hudson River. It was fascinating to watch the movements of boats on the water and helicopters through the air as they made their way to, from, and around the statue's island.

The best time to enjoy these views was evening, as the sun went down. The blue sky gradually faded into varying shades of orange and pink. The sun would dip behind the distant landscape of the New Jersey shore. The sharp definition of bridges, buildings, and traffic gradually faded into an awe-inspiring backdrop of lights: from the red, white, and blue glow on the top third of the Empire State Building, to the orange glow of sodium street lamps, to the bright whites of the offices where night owls toiled, keeping the finances of the world flowing in 24/7 continuity. New York City by night is like nowhere else on earth. And there existed no better place to see those lights than from the unobstructed view on top of the north tower of the World Trade Center. Tourists visiting the observation deck of the south tower, on the other hand, had the north tower's bulk to contend with in their gaze toward midtown.

Amanda spent many an evening at Windows on the World, trying to find an anchor for her life and cope with the pain of a difficult past. She describes herself as "not the most worthy person in town." The servers came to recognize her and adopted her as though she were one of the staff. They kept an eye on her, warding off the wrong kind of males. If she had had too much to drink as closing time approached, one or more servers would escort her to the parking lot in the basement, drive her home, and make sure that she made it into her apartment safely. The service staff at Windows on the World gradually became family to her.

Somewhat surprisingly, she had never brought a camera with her to the restaurant. She would describe the massive towers and the incredible views to far-flung family and acquaintances, but she never got around to actually collecting photos. After enduring repeated requests, she finally promised her mother that she would take some day-time pictures the week of September 10.

When she heard that servers were being called in for special preparations on the morning of September 11, she decided to take advantage of her relationship with them to get some early-morning pictures out the restaurant windows. She agreed to be there at 8:30 a.m., 10 floors above and 16 minutes before the impact of American Airlines Flight 11. Amanda had no idea that a simple request from her mother was the equivalent of a death warrant. Of the 1,432 civilians (not counting police, fire, and other building personnel) who died in the north tower, 1,360 were in the upper part from the ninety-second through the 110th floor.

On the morning of September 11 Amanda woke with a start at 8:40 a.m. She was stunned when she looked at the clock, because she doesn't normally oversleep. It was a beautiful sunny day, and she was amazed that she hadn't stirred earlier. Feeling confused as to what to do, since she had already missed her appointment to get into the restaurant, she lay there a while trying to decide her next move. Fifteen minutes later her phone rang.

"Amanda, where are you, where are you?" the frantic voice of a friend from New Jersey shrilled.

"Where am I? I'm right here. Where am I supposed to be?" Amanda felt even more confused, wondering what on earth was wrong with her friend.

"Where *are* you?" demanded the voice once again.

"I'm right here, in my apartment. In fact, I am lying in bed. Why do you want to know?"

"Aren't you supposed to be at the World Trade Center right now?"

"Yes; I overslept."

"Thank God, thank God, thank God!" her friend began to sob, "I thought you were dead!"

"What do you mean, dead?" Amanda asked.

"Are you sure you're actually in your apartment right now?"

"Of course I'm sure. What's going on?" By now Amanda was starting to get a little upset with her friend.

"You don't know what happened? You'd better turn on your TV. A plane just crashed into your restaurant" [actually a few floors below].

Not really comprehending the impossible, Amanda staggered over to the TV, rubbing a throbbing head and brushing long black hair away from her face. She turned it on just in time to catch the image of the north tower smoldering as United Airlines Flight 175 exploded into the south tower. As she realized that many of her friends were trapped above the flames in the north tower she found herself seized by the same panic that had motivated her friend to call.

"I'm fine, I'm fine, but please hang up. I need to try to get through to the restaurant and see if everyone is OK." Immediately Amanda dialed Windows on the World, but the phone was busy. She dialed another number she knew, but nothing happened. Then she looked up the cell phones of a couple servers at the restaurant, but the calls didn't go through. Seized with fear and pain, she was transfixed by the images on the screen until one by one the two towers collapsed, and her hopes with them. Twenty-three servers that she knew by name and face never went home that day. It was as if she had lost her whole extended family in a moment.

Like George Sleigh, Amanda has often wondered why she was spared that day when so many of her friends perished. She doesn't think of herself as "the most worthy person." In fact, she has done many things in life that she regrets. On the other hand, the staff of the restaurant was a caring group who treated her as a "worthy person," even though she didn't feel she deserved it. She told me that they had treated her better than she would have treated them if the roles had been reversed.

Nevertheless, Amanda truly believes that her having overslept that day was an act of God. It was just not normal for her. She believes that God saved her on September 11 and that it was a call to a new level of commitment to Him and to right living. But why her? Why did God go out of His way to preserve her life when so many "worthier" people lost their lives that day? What did that say about God?

The House of Mercy

The Bible contains a dramatic example of God's inscrutable but tender mercies. It is the story of a man paralyzed for 38 years, who spent his time at a place where people were supposed to get well. I have recounted the man's experience below but you can read the biblical account for yourself in chapter 5 of the New Testament book of John.

Paralyzed at the Edge

A crippled man lay on a mat beside a pool in Jerusalem. Rumor had it that every so often an angel came down and stirred the waters of the pool. The first one into the pool after the water rippled would be cured of whatever disease he or she had. Huge crowds came to the place to be healed, so much so that at times the man couldn't even *see* the pool from where he lay. The least trembling of the water often resulted in a stampede. On one occasion a couple people had been trampled to death in the process. For years now the man had watched the water, waiting for a chance to be healed, but whenever the surface rippled, someone less sick than he would jump in first. It was hopeless. As the years went by the man's eyes glazed over in despair more and more often. The paralysis of body was becoming a paralysis of mind.

As time dragged on he sometimes allowed himself a few moments of regret. During his youth he had engaged in some highly risky behaviors; sin, the rabbis had called it. They had warned him that sin would lead to sickness and death, and in his case it had—a living death! What kind of emptiness had pushed him to continue in such destructive behaviors? Had he known the consequences of his actions, would he have quit in time? Thirty-eight years of suffering. Was it fair? Did he really deserve this?

But even worse than the paralysis was the rejection. Because his sickness was the consequence of his sinful actions, most people, especially the religious ones, had spurned him. Abandoned to his fate, he remained all alone, imprisoned with his thoughts, and they were no fun at all. Suddenly a kind face bent over him and broke through his glazed stare. He recognized in that face the compassion of a man who knew what it was like to suffer rejection. Beyond that, he saw interest and concern. "Do you want to get well?" the man asked.

What kind of question is that? the crippled man thought. *Do I want to get well? Does a drowning man want air? Does a Roman want power? Who is this guy, anyway?*

The biblical story of the crippled man by the Pool of Bethesda is fairly well known. Paralyzed for 38 years, he had been a regular at the pool for a long time. According to John 5, Jesus arrived at the pool on a Sabbath day, picked the man out of the crowd, and healed him instantly. Aspects of the story have some relevance to the matter of who died and who didn't on September 11.

The name *Bethesda* meant "House of Mercy," but the hundreds who sought healing there received little mercy (John 5:1-3). Although the King James Version of the Bible states that an angel of the Lord stirred up the healing waters, the older biblical manuscripts leave out that element of the story. It would certainly have been strange for God to arrange a healing mechanism that favored the least sick (thus more mobile) over the truly needy. After all, what hope does a paralyzed man have in a race with people who have anything from a head cold to a shoulder injury? While there are many things we don't know about this pool, we know that in this story, Jesus shows mercy at the very place where people looked for mercy.

The man seems to have been totally abandoned (verse 7). Having no friends or family to help him in his quest for healing, he was truly a hopeless case. The system had nothing more to offer him, yet he clung to it for lack of any other option. Perhaps Jesus specifically selected him because he was the most pitiful of all the cases available. Jesus seems to have used the incident as an acted illustration of what He states in verse 21—that He can give life to anyone He wishes, and that His life-giving power has no limits.

Jesus' action and statement assert God's freedom to intervene in human affairs when and how He chooses. Jesus picked one man out of a whole crowd of people. The paralytic hadn't sought Him out, didn't even know Him, and had expressed no faith in Him before being healed (verses 6-9, 13). Nor was he young, so you couldn't argue that Jesus chose him because of his potential. Nor did he have a long track record of usefulness and experience either, having been paralyzed for 38 years. The man wasn't the religious type (see verse 14), nor did he have influential friends or family to argue in his behalf (verse 7). We find no record that after his healing he even thanked Jesus. Instead he turned Him in to the hostile authorities (verses 15, 16). Nothing about this man would single him out as worthy of special attention.

It reminds me of so many people, such as Amanda, who were rescued on September 11 or who were away from the towers for arbitrary or inexplicable reasons. While they don't know why, and often feel unworthy, they are absolutely certain that God directly intervened in their lives, that they are alive for a purpose. I believe God does things like this, not to excuse problematic or sinful behavior, but so people can experience His grace and thereby take courage to seek a relationship with Him.

The Problem With Miracles

In the March 21, 2002, issue of *Adventist Review*, Stephen Chavez reflected on the arbitrary nature of the events of September 11 and what that had to say about God. Chavez stated that miracles have two problems. For one thing, it is hard to tell the difference between a miracle and a coincidence. If a commuter plane goes down, killing half the passengers, how many of the survivors were saved miraculously and how many escaped death simply because they were sitting in the "right" section of the plane? No doubt those who lived would be inclined to consider their survival a miracle.

Which raises a second problem with miracles. Why didn't God miraculously preserve *everyone's* life? Or to put it another way, why would Jesus heal one man in a crowd of sick people, leave the rest where they were, and then never return to the pool (as far as we know)? Tragedy is difficult enough to take by itself. But the preservation of even one person in the midst of slaughter, as wondrous as that may be, serves as the frame for a giant question mark regarding the loss of so many.

The tragedies of September 11 killed thousands and spared even more thousands. We see no detectable pattern among the saved or the lost that would offer any explanation. Sometimes it was as simple as who got up and who slept in, or who was located on the ninety-first floor and who on the ninety-second. Chavez concludes by suggesting that survivors need to be careful how they celebrate miracles. "Not everyone survives a terminal illness or an automobile accident; not every lost child (tool, dog, wallet, watch) is found."

The Story of Job

On September 11 Sister Regina Palamara spoke to residents of Roosevelt Island near Manhattan at the start of a nondenominational prayer service held at the Chapel of the Good Shepherd. She told them that in 10 years of praying at the chapel, she had never seen or heard anything like what she had witnessed a few minutes earlier, just before the prayer meeting began. A man had walked up the aisle, knelt down, raised his arms, and yelled at God for more than 15 minutes. "I witnessed someone really experience the prayer of Job," she recalled, ". . . the man who has nothing left." Concerned, she called public safety officers, who stood by, then later escorted the man out of the chapel.

The man's name was Anthony Deligia. He had witnessed the carnage at the World Trade Center earlier in the day, then had walked to Roosevelt Island with a colleague who lived there. "I worked on a U.S. military submarine from 1980 to 1992," Deligia said. "I slept on missiles and realized that 15 minutes was all it took to blow everything away. I left the service when the cold war ended, and I thought that really was the end of the war. Today I saw it start again."

Since his release from the military, the 43-year-old Deligia had worked as a Unix programmer for a Japanese bank located on the fiftieth floor of one of the now-demolished World Trade Center towers. He said he saw women with their skin peeling off as he descended 49 floors to the street. "Once I got outside, I saw people jump out of the building. They looked like toys falling into a ball of smoke. It was unreal, like a game," Deligia reported. "I am angry with God, who let all this happen."

As hinted by Sister Regina, the Bible does not leave the issue of tragedy and suffering unaddressed. The biblical story about a man named Job, drawn up in the genre of a Hebrew play, wrestles with the issue of why bad things happen to good people (Psalm 73 addresses the reverse issue of why good things happen to bad people). This story has had such an impact on the world that even in today's secular environment, nearly everyone has heard of "the patience of Job."

The story begins in the land of Uz (Job 1). Job was a very wealthy man, perhaps the richest in the world. But his greatest treasure was his children, seven sons and three daughters. Every morning before the sun rose he prayed that God would protect them through the day. But one day, as Job prayed, his case came up in the heavenly court, although he was not aware of it.

Satan, the prince of evil and darkness, slipped into the heavenly court with a crowd of "the sons of God." After noting his presence, God offered Satan a challenge. "Have you noticed my servant Job? He worships me faithfully and is careful to do nothing wrong."

"Big deal," Satan countered. "He's into religion for what he can get. You've given him everything. No wonder he worships You. But mark my words. Take away all he has and he'll curse You to Your face!"

"OK, we'll see," God responded. "Everything he has is in your hands. Just don't hurt Job himself."

The scene moves back to earth, where one disaster after another falls on Job's estate. Bandits, fire, marauding armies, and storms destroy Job's animals, servants, and possessions, and eventually even his children, leaving him destitute and childless in a moment. Job's response? He falls on the ground, worships God, and says, "Naked I came from my mother's womb, and naked I will depart. The Lord gave and the Lord has taken away; may the name of the Lord be praised" (Job 1:21).

When the heavenly court reconvened, God pointed out to Satan that Job's faithfulness had not diminished despite the great losses he had experienced. But the great accuser hadn't finished yet.

"Big deal," he exclaimed. "Skin for skin! A man will give all he has for his own life. But stretch out Your hand and strike his flesh and bones, and he will surely curse You to Your face."

God met Satan's insinuation by placing Job in the devil's control, with only one limitation. Satan must spare Job's life. So the accuser afflicts Job with loathsome and painful sores from head to toe. Even his wife turns against him and urges him to "curse God and die." But Job does not remain alone. Three "friends" hear about his troubles and come to console him.

This begins a long section of the story in which Job's friends try to convince him that God is not arbitrary (Job 4:7-11; 15:17-35). If things have gone wrong for Job, he must somehow be to blame for it (Job 8:1-22; 15:5, 6; 22:1-11). The Lord is trying to get Job's attention (Job 5:17-27). So if he would just turn to God and humble himself, things would get better (Job 22:21-30), but if he blamed God for his troubles, he would end up just like the wicked (Job 11:13-20). Great friends!

In response, Job denied the charges, crying out to God to be a friend in his emptiness (Job 7:7-21). He insisted that he is an exception to the rule that suffering is the consequence of sin, that he is innocent of anything that would justify his great losses (Job 6:24-30; 13:13-23; 31:1-40). Under harassment from his friends (Job 6:14-23), he began to accuse God of injustice and oppression (Job 9:13-35;

10:1-22; 27:1-6). Job railed at God's silence (Job 23:1-9; 29:2-5) and mocked his friends' theological arguments (Job 12:2, 3; 13:4, 5,12; 16:1-3). Their theories that good always receives its reward and evil always get punished just don't square with reality (Job 24:1-25). In the real world the wicked prosper and the righteous die (Job 21:7-34). And God sits there and watches it all (Job 28:24). Job wishes he had never been born (Job 3:1-19).

After a lengthy and at times tedious debate covering 29 chapters in the book of Job, the four men fall silent and a fifth appears, named Elihu. He has been listening respectfully, but now he cannot hold his feelings back any longer (Job 32:6-10, 18-22). Although he is human, he has come to speak in defense of God. Elihu starts out by mocking the failure of Job's friends to convince him that he is wrong (Job 32:11-17). He then goes after Job directly. The sufferer was wrong to accuse God of being silent. God is not silent; human beings just don't pay attention (Job 33:14-18). Pain is one way God uses to get people's attention (verses 19-28). God never does the wrong thing. He gives people only what they deserve (Job 34:1-15). Even suffering has a purpose— it is a discipline that the Lord uses to teach those He loves (Job 36:22, 23). Thus God is far from being silent. He is present whenever it rains, whenever the thunder roars or the lightning strikes (Job 36:24-33; 37:1-20)!

As if on cue, a mighty thunderstorm approaches the small group of men. Elihu seems to recognize the presence of God in the storm (Job 37:21, 22). And sure enough, God speaks out of the storm and addresses Job and Job alone (38:1–42:6). At first God seems to support all that the four companions of Job have said to him. He accuses Job of questioning Him with ignorant, empty words. Then He throws a series of unanswerable questions the man's way. "Where were you when I made the world? You know so much, tell me about it. Have you ever commanded a day to dawn? Have you ever walked the floor of the ocean? Can you guide the stars from year to year, or change their orbits? Do you gather food for the lions? Did you teach the hawk how to fly?" And so on.

After Job admits his ignorance for the first time, God pelts him with another series of unanswerable questions. "Can you tie up a whale like a pet bird? Are you trying to put Me in the wrong so you can be right?" Job offers the only possible response to overwhelming rightness and power. "Surely I spoke of things I did not understand, things too wonderful for me to know," he replies plaintively (Job 42:3). "My ears had heard of you but now my eyes have seen you. Therefore I despise myself and repent in dust and ashes" (verses 5, 6). God doesn't answer any of Job's questions; rather He asks him a string of His own. Nevertheless, Job's attitude has totally changed. Out of his new understanding and relationship with God he becomes satisfied that God is just. Knowing *about* God is not the answer to his questions. But *knowing* God is.

Then a fascinating thing happens. God turns from Job to his three "friends" and declares that He is angry with them because they didn't tell the truth about Him, as Job had done (verses 7-9)! The statement is startling, of course, since Job has just endured nearly four chapters' worth of rebuke himself. The story winds down to a strange and puzzling conclusion (verses 10-17).

What was God doing on September 11? On the surface the book of Job offers no answer, only more questions. The arguments of Job and his friends sound familiar, but they do not satisfy (especially when you know they have absolutely nothing to do with what actually happened between God and Satan). Then Elihu comes along and criticizes both Job and his three friends, yet says many of the same things they have charged! Finally God rebukes Job for speaking out of ignorance, only to end up telling his friends that they were wrong and the sufferer right!

So anyone who comes to this biblical drama expecting all the answers to the problem of suffering will likely be disappointed. Job's friends are full of answers, many of them still offered today, but all of the answers get mocked at some point in the book. When God appears, He presents no answers, just a sense of His overpowering greatness.

Perhaps the main point of the book is that none of the general answers to the problem of suffering had anything to do with why Job was suffering. The real reason involved a struggle between God and Satan in the heavenly court. No statement in the earth-centered part of the book (chapters 3-42) ever returns to that issue, not even the statements of God Himself. So the point of the book seems to be that the limited context of human experience does not allow a satisfying intellectual answer to the problem of suffering. We just don't have the context to understand, even if the one doing the explaining is God Himself.

Don't get me wrong here. I'm not saying that our lives on this earth are hostage to cosmic wagers God is making out there somewhere. After all, Job is not a detailed explanation of divine ways. But the point of the story is that our lives are affected by wider issues in the universe as a whole, things that don't make sense from the perspective of a single planet alone. God's will is not always done on this earth. As the Lord asserts in the book of Job, to try to explain September 11, the Holocaust, and similar events is like commanding a day to dawn, roping a whale, or walking on the floor of the ocean. It is just not a realistic enterprise for humans confined to the limited context of our world.

Why then did God's response satisfy Job even though it was not a real answer? If nothing else, it was because the Lord cared enough to speak to him. After all, if God answered all of Job's questions, how could the story comfort those who don't receive any answers to their questions? But as it stands, his story can encourage those still left in the dark. While Job doesn't get any explanation from God, he does encounter Him, and that is enough. To know God is to trust Him. The real reason for suffering remains hidden in God's heart. Job's foolishness, as pointed out in God's speech at the end, was the assumption that if he couldn't come up with a reason for his suffering, the Lord didn't have one either.

Perhaps the best news in the book of Job is that undeserved suffering will not last forever. It ended for Job, and it will one day cease for the human race as a whole. To paraphrase Shakespeare: "The earth is like a stage and we are merely players." One day God will reveal a much bigger picture.

But that is not the end of the story. The book of Job is not the Bible's last word on the matter of suffering. We see a much more decisive response to the issue in the New Testament. According to the Gospels, there was another day that changed the world, a day whose reverberations have continued to travel down through history to our own time.

SOURCES

Cauchon, Dennis. "For Many on Sept. 11 Survival Was No Accident." *USA Today,* Dec. 19, 2001.

Chavez, Stephen. "The Problem With Miracles." *Adventist Review,* Mar. 21, 2002, p. 5.

Shrivastava, Anusha. "In a Chapel Gathering, Residents Share Grief." *The Main Street Wire,* Sept. 13, 2001.

8

THE DAY THAT CHANGED THE WORLD

One Friday in Jerusalem

Almost 2,000 years ago there was a Friday in Jerusalem that changed the world. All the elements of September 11 occurred within the experience of a single person, but that incident had implications that affect every person who has ever lived. As I did with September 11, let me start by telling the story of what happened that day through the eyes of several witnesses. In this case we find the story recorded in the biblical books of Matthew, Mark, Luke, and John. Hollywood productions such as *The Robe, Ben-Hur, The Greatest Story Ever Told,* and *Jesus of Nazareth* have featured various aspects of the account.

The story of that Friday actually began on Thursday night. Jesus celebrated the Jewish Passover with His disciples. He then walked with them down the steep staircase of a street that led from the upper part of Jerusalem to the Kidron Valley south and east of the city. As they headed down the hill the men would have concentrated on the placement of their feet, because of the unevenness of the steps.

Night had fallen, but it was still early. The stairstep street was largely dark, but the occasional house torch supplemented the light of the torches a couple disciples had brought along. The air was probably a bit chilly on a March evening at Jerusalem's elevation. Every so often a gap in the buildings to the left would have allowed a glimpse of the brightly lit Temple, looking ever larger and more imposing as they worked their way eastward down the hill. When buildings blocked the view of the Temple, they became sil-houetted shadows against the yellow glow of the night sky.

After a few hundred yards Jesus and the disciples reached the bottom of Mount Zion and headed up the small rise to the top of Ophel Ridge, just south of the Temple. To the left was the giant marble staircase that Jesus and the disciples had used many times to enter the Temple court-yard. But that night Jesus showed no interest in the Temple. He was heading elsewhere. Soon the group went out the Water Gate and down the steep, winding path from the Ophel Ridge to the Kidron Valley.

From there they headed north up the valley until the Temple was once more above and to the left, while in front of them and to the right was the Mount of Olives. Jesus led the disciples to a favorite spot for prayer, in an olive grove just east of Jerusalem.

When they arrived at the garden Jesus left eight of the disciples at the entrance as if to guard the place. He took John, Peter, and James with Him for a ways, then went on a bit farther to pray alone. The disciples soon fell asleep. Jesus began to agonize as He anticipated the events He was about to experience. Three times He sought comfort from His disciples, but each time He found them asleep.

According to the Bible, Jesus' agony had little to do with the physical suffering He would experience the next day. Rather, as the "God-man" He was designated to expe-rience all the consequences of human evil in His own per-son. His death on the cross would sum up all the pain, all the suffering, all the regret, and all the rejection that evil has caused the human race. Jesus would endure loss of meaning, loss of relationship, and all the misery of human sickness and death (Isaiah 53:1-12). His anguish was much more mental and emotional than physical.

At this point in the story Judas arrives with a small

crowd of Temple police and people who have followed them out of the city, many of them carrying swords and clubs. They are searching for Jesus to arrest Him. But Jesus is no longer assailed with anguish. He has made His decision to accept what lies ahead, and from here on His actions are decisive and purposeful. As the mob meets Jesus, He steps forward boldly and identifies Himself. One of His disciples, Peter, draws his sword to defend Jesus, but Jesus orders him to put it away and allow Him to be captured (Matthew 26:52). When the disciples see that Jesus is not resisting arrest, they all flee for their own lives, although two of them, Peter and John, follow events from a distance.

After His arrest, the religious authorities take Jesus for immediate trial before the high priests of the national religion, Annas and Caiaphas. Due process seems not to be a concern at Jesus' trial. False witnesses give their "testimony," although disagreements among them mitigate its value to the accusers. The Roman occupying power uses torture to try to extract a confession from Jesus. During the course of His various trials, He gets slapped in the face, beaten with rods, whipped with long cords, mocked, and derided. Soldiers spit in His face and press a "crown" of thorns into His head. No one reads Jesus His Miranda rights. It is "terrorism by committee."

The religious authorities in charge of the trial have already decided that they want Jesus put to death. But since they do not have the power to impose the death penalty, they need to convince the Roman authorities that Jesus is a serious threat to them. So they bump Jesus' case over to the Roman governor. The priests at first formulate the charge in political terms for the governor's benefit. They accuse Jesus of forbidding the payment of taxes to Rome (the opposite of what He has actually taught) and of declaring Himself to be a king, therefore a rival to Caesar, the head of Rome. If true, the charges point to serious treason against the Empire.

Pilate interrogates Jesus personally. "Are you the King of the Jews?" he asks. In other words, does Jesus pose a threat to the stability of the government Pilate serves?

Jesus' response is instructive for a post-September 11 world. "My kingdom is not of this world. If it were, my servants would fight to prevent my arrest by the Jews. But now my kingdom is from another place" (John 18:36). As evidence for His assertion Jesus offers the convincing argument of the behavior of His followers at the time of His arrest. If He had been a political revolutionary, His disciples would have fought to the death to prevent His arrest.

Although apparently convinced by Jesus' argument, Pilate wants to make sure that He has understood what Jesus is saying. So he asks for clarification: "You *are* a king, then!" (verse 37).

"You are right in saying I am a king," Jesus replies. "In fact, for this reason I was born, and for this I came into the world, to testify to the truth. Everyone on the side of truth listens to me" (verse 37). His kingdom is a spiritual one, concerned with truth, rather than with political, economic, and military power.

In this exchange we see the strong contrast between Jesus and Muhammad. Jesus regarded it as inappropriate to mix spiritual matters with political and military ones. For Muhammad the material jihad was a major tool for propagating the faith. To Jesus faith was not to be the basis for slaughter, even as a defensive measure, while for Muhammad jihad was always appropriate in defense of faith. Thus Osama bin Laden and Mohamed Atta could consider themselves good, even superior, Muslims. But it would be laughable in the extreme to think of Adolf Hitler as a good Christian.

Convinced that he had settled the matter, Pilate went

out to render judgment, declaring, "I find no basis for a charge against him" (John 19:4). But in response, the religious leaders made it clear they wanted Jesus dead at any cost. While Pilate had right on his side at this point, he was politically vulnerable. He had alienated the Jews in the past, and the emperor had warned him not to allow any more sacrilege against the Jewish religion.

Seeing an opportunity, the religious leaders reversed the charge. Instead of claiming that Jesus threatened Rome, they accused Him of being a blasphemer against their religion. Pilate must act in order to protect their faith from sacrilege. After some consideration he decided to cement his political position by sending an innocent man to death by crucifixion.

Crucifixion was a peculiarly Roman form of execution. Victims had to carry their own crosses in public places as a warning to others. Some people were nailed to the cross; others tied with ropes. The key element, however, was that in order to continue to breathe, its victims had to force themselves up into a certain position, an effort that soon exhausted them. Death usually resulted from suffocation when they could no longer do it. Such death was deliberately slow and painful. An additional element of torture was that of shame and exposure, of hanging naked in public and in all kinds of weather.

Arriving at Golgotha, the place of execution, the Roman soldiers nailed Jesus through His wrists and ankles to the cross and put Him on display between two common thieves. Three hours later He was dead, more from emotional and spiritual anguish than from physical causes. The Roman soldiers, disinterested experts in judging such matters, verified His death. Throughout history some have tried to claim that Jesus did not truly die, but went into a comatose state from which the disciples revived Him. But the best records we have leave no question that He was truly dead that Friday afternoon. Rich friends then secured His body and placed it in a cave tomb nearby, closed off behind a rolling-stone door.

The story reached a climax about 36 hours later, early Sunday morning. Several women decided to visit the tomb and anoint Jesus' body with spices to show Him honor even in death. But when they arrived at the tomb, the stone had been moved away and the tomb was empty. They saw one or two men standing nearby in dazzling apparel (one witness calls them angels). The men told the women not to seek the living among the dead. Jesus had risen from the grave and would appear to His disciples again.

The Central Event of History

For the followers of Jesus that Friday in Jerusalem was, more than any other, the day that changed the world. Jesus' death was more than just the execution of an innocent man. God designed it to unite the human race and ultimately the entire universe (John 12:32; Colossians 1:20).

This is, perhaps, the fundamental difference between Islam and the teachings of Jesus as recorded in the Bible. For Muslims, Jesus is a great prophet who spoke for God, but He is merely a very good man. But according to the Bible, Jesus is much more than a man as well as much more than a prophet. He is God come to earth, but in disguise, cloaked in a human body (John 1:1-14). His mission did not end in a tomb, but continues to change the world today. The relevance of Jesus' mission to our search for God is directly proportional to the reality of that claim.

C. S. Lewis, the great British scholar and novelist, perhaps best explained this central aspect of Christian faith. According to his book *Mere Christianity*, Christians believe that behind events such as September 11 is a universal war between the principles of good and evil. It is a civil war, and rebel forces hold our world hostage. Evil exists here because the world is enemy-occupied territory. On the other hand, the good we see in the world offers evidence that God has not abandoned it to the enemy. He continues to exert His influence with any who are willing to follow Him.

How did evil enter the universe? Lewis argues that God created beings with free will. If we are free to be good, we are also free to be bad. So free will has made evil possible, even though God did not choose to create evil. But why then would He make people free? Because the same freedom that makes evil possible is also the only thing that makes love, joy, or goodness truly worth having. True happiness can occur only in the context of loving choice. Evidently God thought that the pluses of freedom were well worth the risk.

But what if God's creatures used their freedom to go the wrong way, producing unspeakable horrors such as September 11? What then? Does this mean God Himself is evil or perhaps powerless? The Bible says no to both options. Evil exists not because God is a tyrant, but because He prefers openness and freedom. And evil results not from divine powerlessness, but because He wanted human beings to be powerful in ways that mirrored His own freedom of action.

But what has the Lord done to start overcoming the evil in the world? According to Lewis, God has done several things, each outlined in the Bible. 1. He has endowed humanity with the conscience, an inner sense of right and wrong. 2. He has provided some, from Abraham to Moses to Paul (and perhaps Muhammad and others outside the Christian sphere) with visions and dreams that helped clarify the central issues of good and evil. 3. And through the Old Testament He recorded the story of a people (Israel, the Jewish nation) and the struggles through which

God sought to teach them more clearly about Himself.

But then came something special, something surprising. 4. Among the Jews appeared a man who went around talking as if He were God. He claimed to be able to forgive sins, something only Deity can do. Jesus could not be simply a good man. If a mere man claimed to be God, he could not be a good man. To quote Lewis: "A man who was merely a man and said the sort of things Jesus said would not be a great moral teacher. He would either be a lunatic—on a level with the man who says he is a poached egg—or else he would be the Devil of Hell. You must make your choice. Either this man was, and is, the Son of God: or else a madman or something worse."

So the Muslim picture of Jesus is at odds with His own claims and teaching. If Jesus is merely another prophet, one among many, He is a fraud. But if He is what He claimed to be—God Himself taking on human flesh—then the life, death, and resurrection of Jesus are the greatest events that ever happened in the course of human history. That Friday in Jerusalem would then be *the* day that changed the world.

The Implications of the Cross

I believe that the cross changed the world in at least three ways. First, it revised the way we look at our personal lives, particularly our mistakes and failures. Second, it altered the way we find value and meaning for our lives. And third, it transformed the way we look at suffering and tragedy. We will take up each of these changes in turn.

Turning Your Life Around

According to the Bible human beings are not simply imperfect creatures that need improvement—we are rebels who must lay down our arms. The only way out of our human condition is to acknowledge that we are on the wrong track and allow God to work whatever changes are needed in our lives. This is our ultimate jihad, our ultimate struggle to overcome evil.

But "repentance" is not fun. As the chapter on my own personal jihad illustrated, accepting the reality of our brokenness is something we naturally shy away from. Acknowledging failure is humiliating and repugnant. But it is the necessary path toward redeeming our lives from the downward spiral of the evil that besets us all. It is the only way to bring us into the sunshine of reality. Repentance is simply recognizing the truth about ourselves. The day that changed the world can never change us unless we are willing to be changed, unless we recognize that it is necessary.

The neat thing about God's plan is that He understands what this struggle for authenticity is all about. Through submitting Himself to the humiliation of the cross Jesus experienced the kind of surrender we need. In the Garden of Gethsemane He struggled to give Himself up to God's plan. And the Bible teaches that if we follow Him in His surrender and humiliation, we will also share in His conquest of death and find new life in our present experience (Romans 6:3-6).

September 11 was more than just the work of a few kooks and fanatics—it was a symptom of deeper issues that plague us all. As we have seen, the struggle toward authenticity is not an occasional necessity—it is vital and fundamental because of the human condition, whether we admit it or not.

Our Value Before God

I have already pointed out that a fundamental need of human beings is to have a sense of personal value for who we are. This need struggles with the reality (described in the jihad chapter) that the more we know about ourselves, the more we dislike ourselves and the worse we feel. We require a sense of worth, yet authenticity seems to lower our value. How can we elevate our sense of self-worth without denying the dark realities within? That's where the cross comes in.

How much is a human being worth? It depends on the context. If scientists were to melt me down into the chemicals my body consists of, I understand that I would be worth about $12 (make that $13, since I've gained a little weight). Yet employers value the average American at a much higher level than that, something like $50,000 a year. But suppose you were a great basketball player such as Michael Jordan. Suddenly the value jumps to tens of millions of dollars a year. And if you were the nerdy designer of the software everyone in the world uses, you would be valued at tens of billions of dollars!

You see, we are valued in terms of others. But according to the Bible human value is infinitely higher than the worth we assign to each other. Scripture declares that Jesus was worth the whole universe (He made it), yet He knows all about us and still loves us as we are. His death on the cross established the value of each human person. When the Creator of the universe and everyone in it (including all the great athletes and movie stars that people often worship) decided to die for you and me, it placed an infinite value on our lives. And since the resurrected Jesus will never die again, my value is secure in Him as long as I exist.

So the cross provides a true and stable sense of value. It is what makes the story of that Friday in Jerusalem so very special. The cross is not just another atrocity. Rather, it is about God's willingness to take on human flesh and reveal Himself where we are. Jesus' crucifixion demonstrated the value of the human race in God's eyes. And the cross is the key element of His plan to turn the human race away from evil, hatred, and violence. The original day that changed the world, therefore, provides hope for a better world in the aftermath of September 11.

Religion as we know it has clearly failed. Islam has produced numberless jihads and now suicide terrorists. Its followers have brutally tortured and even executed people who were born into an Islamic society but felt the call of God to grow in their faith (many Islamic countries impose the death penalty on any Muslim who converts to another faith). Christianity, on the other hand, has spawned its Crusades and the Inquisition, and has failed to make much of a difference in such situations as Rwanda and the Holocaust. The Middle Ages in Europe, where Christianity was the dominant faith, represent a nightmare of repression and brutality in the name of Jesus. Now even Jews, fresh from the horrors of the Holocaust, have crushed the legitimate hopes of the Palestinian people, many of whom have lived all their lives in the temporary housing of refugee camps.

Thus it is undeniable that none of the great faiths have lived up to the ideals of their sacred texts. Followers of each have, at one time or another, succumbed to the temptations of earthly power and wealth. Their adherents have prized their own opinions so highly that they have felt justified in destroying individuals who thought differently. After September 11 we must beware of our own personal tendency to judge others, to despise those who think in other ways, to marginalize those who look, talk, and pray differently.

The best hope for our world after September 11 is an authentic walk with God that not only takes the "terrorist within" seriously but sees in others the value that God places on them. If every one of us is flawed yet valuable, all other seekers after God become potential allies in the battle to create a kinder and gentler world. Armed with a clear picture of reality and a sense of our value, we can become change agents in the world. And one Friday in Jerusalem planted the seeds of that transformation.

The Suffering God

The cross is also the New Testament's final answer to the problem of suffering that we began to address in the previous chapter. Christ's crucifixion is the most powerful response to the questions How can I believe in God after September 11? How can I believe in a God who allows thousands of innocent people to suffer when He could have done something to stop it? If God exists and He is good, why doesn't He *do* something at times like that?

Such questions directly relate to what happened to Jesus on the cross. As He was dying His greatest suffering had little to do with physical pain from the spikes through His hands and feet, the thorns piercing His forehead, or the torturous effort to breathe that His crucifixion caused. His greatest agony arose from the apparent absence of God in the midst of His suffering. "My God, my God, why have you forsaken me?" He cried out (Matthew 27:46).

Thus Jesus knows from experience what it is like to endure undeserved suffering and pain. He did not deserve to be whipped, beaten, slapped, and spit upon. Jesus did nothing to deserve a sentence of death, the hostility of a hateful mob, or the torture of crucifixion. To the victims of September 11 the cross says: "God knows. He understands. He has tasted what it is like to suffer without having caused it in some way."

As with the book of Job, the cross offers no definitive answer to the problem of unjust suffering. What it does, however, is offer companionship in suffering. The times when we experience undeserved suffering and pain are like our own Friday in Jerusalem. We may feel as if our experience were unique, as if no one has ever been more alone. But Jesus

Himself went there in depth on the original Good Friday. He understands what it is like to be totally alone, totally rejected and abused. In a real sense He tasted just a bit of everyone's experience (1 Peter 2:20-24).

But for Jesus the story didn't end on that Friday. At first it seemed to, and in the agony of the moment He Himself saw no hope for the future when He cried out to God, "Why have you forsaken me?" But His suffering and apparent abandonment turned out to be a prelude to the incredible affirmation of Easter Sunday. When He was raised from the dead, His acceptance with God was reaffirmed. In some sense the whole human race now stands in a new place with God. The cross has turned human suffering into a prelude to something greater.

What difference does it make to believe in the cross today? For me it changes everything about suffering. Some have used undeserved suffering as an excuse to deny God's existence. But atheism has not lessened human suffering one iota. If anything it makes it worse, because it leaves one all alone in meaninglessness and with no future.

But the cross demonstrates several things that make a difference. It tells us that we are not alone, even though it may feel that way. The Crucifixion declares that suffering doesn't indicate that God doesn't care—He cares ever so much, but He doesn't always intervene to avert pain. God's absence in suffering is not a hostile one or a helpless one, but has a higher purpose. In the light of the cross we have a motivation to endure, even though we may not know the particular reason why. When we suffer without deserving it, we share in the experience of Jesus. And when we do not sense God's presence in our pain, we also share in His experience. He went there before us and understands how we feel.

I remember Paul, the "happy Hungarian," who used to serve as a greeter in my church. The man was amazing. He had a smile for everyone, an encouraging word, a pat on the back, or a hug. There seemed to be no limits to his optimism and his joyful spirit. You never heard him say anything bad about anybody. Never involving himself in church differences, he just kept on smiling and praying through everything.

In his 70s, however, he contracted a deadly form of cancer. If anyone could do battle with cancer through the medicine of laughter and optimism, Paul was the one. But things did not go well. One day I noticed his granddaughter, in her late teens at the time, acting quite depressed, something unusual for her. I asked her what was wrong. She said that her grandfather was clearly dying and that if I wanted to see him once more, I had better visit him in the hospital that week.

When I arrived at the hospital, I somehow expected him to be weak but still his normal self in terms of optimism. It wasn't that way at all, however. He poured out his bitterness and pain. "Why me? Why now?" was the ongoing refrain. This stalwart Christian had lost track of God's presence, and his optimism went with it. Truly confused, I wondered momentarily if I had visited the wrong person. While it was unquestionably him, his spirit had been broken, and I could hardly recognize him as a result.

At first I wondered what I could possibly say that would make any difference in his great hour of need. Then I decided to try something.

"Paul, if I were in your situation, I'm sure I'd feel as upset as you do," I told him.

"I'm sorry I've been such bad company today," he replied. "It really does feel better to share how I feel about it with you."

"Paul, did you know that on the cross Jesus felt the same way as you do?"

He looked surprised. "He did? How do you know?"

"Do you remember what He said on the cross? 'My God, my God, why have you forsaken me?' That tells me He knows how you feel, and that He thought it was OK to challenge God a little. God would rather hear our honest anger than our silence or even sweet words that aren't heartfelt."

"You really think so?" Paul asked.

"That's what the Bible says," I assured him. "It's OK to tell God how you feel, even when you don't feel so good. But you know what I think?"

"What?"

"Now you can also understand what Jesus experienced on the cross. He didn't deserve to suffer and die any more than you do. What He went through wasn't right, but He endured, knowing that it would turn out all right in the end. If nothing else, you are having a share in the suffering He went through. You can understand Him in a way that I can't, with all my study and training. If God is allowing you to go through this, then He must know that the ultimate good will outweigh the present evil."

We continued the conversation for a while along the same lines, and then he said, "You know what? Today you taught me something. All I could think about was me. But now I know better how Jesus felt. And I know He understands what I'm going through. Anything that helps me know God better is worth it." Now a changed man, he relaxed back against the pillow with a slight smile and a look of peace on his face. You don't always have to know why as long as you know you are not alone.

The Ultimate Act of Terrorism

Why September 11 and similar tragedies in the course of history? There is no satisfactory answer at this time. Yet it is possible to discern a merciful hand in the events, in spite of their horrific nature. The toll at the World Trade Center could easily have been in the tens of thousands dead—if the planes had arrived a few hours later in the day, if they had struck the towers at a lower level, if the towers had collapsed more quickly, if evacuations hadn't started so quickly and efficiently in the south tower. As horrible as events were, it could have been—in a sense *should* have been—much worse.

For those of us who experienced it, September 11 was an unimaginable expression of evil at its worst. It fundamentally altered our perception of the world and our own role in it. But September 11 was not the most evil act of all time. Nor was the Holocaust, as chillingly brutal and unfair as it was. The Inquisition, the Crusades, the genocides of Armenians, Russians, Rwandans, and Cambodians in the twentieth century, the slave trade across the Atlantic—all of them represent acts of systematic premeditated evil. But none of them qualify as the ultimate evil deed.

The cross was the most evil act of all time. When human beings, for temporary and limited political advantage, crucified the God who came down and lived among us, they acted in the most incomprehensible, unfair, and evil manner possible. In rejecting Him, they did more than just condemn an innocent man to death—they destroyed the source of their own life and repudiated their own place in the universe. The cross of Jesus Christ is an evil deed of infinite proportions. If the human race is capable of that, no evil action is unimaginable.

But the dark cloud of human evil has a silver lining. God has turned the cross into a powerful act of reversal. He has transformed the greatest evil ever committed into the most powerful act of goodness ever performed. By death God brings life. Through defeat comes victory. Shame, humiliation, and rejection have produced glory, grace, and acceptance. God has used the cross to turn the tables on evil and death. The greatest evil has become the basis for the greatest good.

That suggests to me that all the good that has come as a result of September 11 is not just an accident. God's hand was there, guiding, saving, helping even in the midst of tragedy, suffering, and death. As a result of this evil act, millions of people have made fresh commitments to family and service to others. Many people are turning away from greed, corruption, and empty display. And many who had forgotten God are returning to Him with a passion not seen in decades.

What difference does all this make in practical terms? If you live in the United States, you know that people find themselves torn between two tasks in the wake of September 11. Authorities tell us to go about our lives "as if nothing has happened or will happen," yet they constantly warn us to be vigilant or everything we have can be blown to smithereens in the next moment. Many Americans are perplexed. They don't know how to prepare for future attacks, they don't know how to relax, and they feel helpless.

The cross, however, shows us how to live in conflicted times. Its light demonstrates that there is plenty we can do in the face of terrorism. We can learn to love our neighbors the way God does. We can help to build bridges between groups in our communities. We can make a daily effort to project love and care into the world, and not return evil for evil. We can visit the sick, feed the hungry, and comfort the suffering. And we can even learn to love our enemies the way Jesus did! The cross reveals that the grace and power that come only from God can transform evil into good.

The cross was a day of great terror, and many who saw it ran away dismayed about what was happening. The person who had healed others, who banished disease and hunger wherever He walked, who gave love and hope to downtrodden multitudes, had been cruelly and unjustly executed.

What if those who watched this senseless act of violence had said, "How can we ever trust God again?" Suppose they had gone home, renounced their belief in Him, and said, "Either God does not exist, or He is a monster that has a complete disregard for love and justice." If they had, they would have missed the greatest act of God's love and justice in human history.

That's why I believe that we can trust Him after September 11. Evil seems to rule only if we don't look carefully or wait long enough. God is still going to use people like you and me to change the world in the aftermath of evil. Wars, violence, and terrorism are born in the heart. But the cross has exposed the fundamental weakness of evil: It can be overcome with good. So I have become willing to fight evil wherever it is found—among "them" (whoever they are), among "us" (whoever we are), but most of all "in here," inside of me. I think it's time to start a new conspiracy in this world, one with a world-changing message: *Evil will be overcome with good*. This is our mission.